LET YOUR CUSTOMERS DO THE TALKING

301 + *Word-of-Mouth* Marketing Tactics Guaranteed To Boost Profits

MICHAEL E. CAFFERKY

UPSTART PUBLISHING
Specializing in Small Business Publishing
a division of Dearborn Publishing Group, Inc.

Executive Editor: Bobbye Middendorf
Managing Editor: Jack Kiburz
Interior Design: Lucy Jenkins
Cover Design: Design Alliance, Inc.

Published by Upstart Publishing Company, Inc.,
a division of Dearborn Publishing Group, Inc.

Printed in the United States of America

96 97 98   10 9 8 7 6 5 4 3 2 1

Library of Congress Cataloging-in-Publication Data
Cafferky, Michael E.
    Let Your Customers Do the Talking : 301+ word-of-mouth marketing tactics guaranteed to boost profits / by Michael E. Cafferky
        p. cm.
    Includes index.
    ISBN 0-936894-95-4 (pbk.)
    1. Marketing.   2. Word-of-mouth advertising.   3. Consumer satisfaction
4. Customer services.   I. Title.
HF5415.122.C33   1996
658,8--dc20   95-32139
                                                                    CIP

To Marlene

*A*cknowledgments

*T*he material in this book has been gathered from a variety of perspectives, the most important being the reports from many businesses of what actually works. I am grateful for the many businesses, both large and small, that have shown the power of word of mouth through their examples.

I thank my family—Marlene, Bryan, Nolan—for their support and encouragement during the research and development of my word-of-mouth marketing training programs and this book.

I acknowledge the contributions of my students in Principles of Marketing and Marketing Management courses at La Sierra University School of Business & Management, who showed enthusiasm for the material on word-of-mouth marketing.

I am grateful for the friendship and encouragement of John Healy, Patti Hillis and Frank Buono, of the Wrigley Village Business Association in Long Beach, California.

I am also grateful to the following individuals, who spent their valuable time talking with me about the word-of-mouth dynamics of their businesses and who have given permission to profile their companies in this book:

Fred Anderson, Anderson Landscaping
Kim Anderson, Anderson Construction

James Armel, Prudential California Realty
Barry Fribush, Bubbling Bath Spa & Tub
Lynn Gordon, French Meadow Bakery
Patti Hillis, Pete's Plumbing
Howdy Holmes, Chelsea Milling Company
Sally D. Jackson, founding partner, Boston Beer Company, and president of Jackson & Company, the brewery's public relations agency
Karen Lippe, Seven Crown Resorts
Bruce Parker, Callaway Golf Company
Malcolm Smith, Malcolm Smith Motor Sports

$\mathcal{C}$ontents

*P*reface

"The way to gain a good reputation is to endeavor to be what you desire to appear."

— Socrates

*O*ne evening a country music star drove into a small Texas town and stopped at the only honky-tonk for miles. He went in and had a short conversation with the manager. A few minutes later this popular musician began entertaining the few patrons. Word of the free concert passed faster than a prairie fire. The place was packed within half an hour.

This example shows the sheer power of high-velocity word of mouth. In contrast, most successful word-of-mouth programs create slower, steadier growth. However, businesses *can* experience significant results within the span of a few weeks, as the following example attests.

As a volunteer with the Long Beach Business Consulting Service, I was referred to a client who needed new customers fast. His new company served the trucking industry near the harbor, but not many truckers knew about his services. To complicate matters, three strong competitors with established clientele also served the area, and the only periodical for truckers had an exclusive advertising agreement with one of them.

Together we designed a tactical plan whereby he would meet the business owners and managers of companies nearby that also provided products and services to truck drivers. He offered to give a complimentary service for their personal vehicles. He also asked if they could recommend him to truckers.

Within a few days, truck drivers began arriving. His schedule started to fill up. Cash flow increased. When I called three weeks later, he told me he didn't have time to talk because he had customers waiting. Three months later, his business was still growing. This kind of marketing power is available to thousands of other types of businesses, too.

Word of mouth has historically been the chief means to signal value to customers, a dynamic used in enterprise for centuries. In the last 50 years, studies have codified the principles, roots, causes and usefulness so that you can consciously and systematically apply the concepts of word-of-mouth marketing.

Let Your Customers Do the Talking can help you create a simple plan to build your business using just one powerful resource: your reputation in your community. Your reputation among satisfied customers is your most valuable marketing resource, something that cannot be purchased as part of a media blitz. It's about winning confidence, building trust and instilling gratitude in clients and in others who are your loyal supporters.

If you are like every business professional I have ever known, you want to build your business through the power of your positive reputation. Using the principles in this book, this is something you can plan for and make a reality.

You will find more than 300 specific activities listed here that have produced truly satisfying and profitable results for a wide range of businesses. You will also learn the secrets of how and why word of mouth works so you can start applying the basic principles to any situation right away.

In addition, I have provided practical, useful resources for

- identifying the clients who will build your reputation.
- costing out word-of-mouth marketing.
- networking to build your referrals.
- building your reputation across cultures.
- preventing negative word of mouth.
- tapping into the infrastructure of your client's industry.
- using the power of business ethics and emotions to build word of mouth.
- introducing new products and services with word of mouth.

- blending word of mouth with other methods of signaling value to customers.
- identifying 53 opportunities when word-of-mouth marketing pays immediate dividends.

While most of the ideas in this book can be implemented with a small staff on a low budget, large, multinational companies will also find them valuable. Advertising agencies, public relations firms and marketing consultants will find this book helpful as they develop new promotional campaigns for their clients. Sales organizations will find the methods of some of the most successful salespeople in America. Business owners and executives will find the "how-to" behind the secret formula for success used by the best and fastest-growing companies in the world. Coupled with the power of paid advertising, word of mouth will make your work more efficient and more profitable. Word-of-mouth marketing is not free: It does cost time and, more important, your commitment.

Other books assume that your primary mode of promotion is paid advertising. However, this book will show you that word-of-mouth marketing is the best foundation upon which to build all your other promotional efforts. Paid advertising is an important means to obtain customer response, but your reputation is built primarily by the referrals your champion customers make for you when they recommend your products and services to others.

Joining a networking club can be helpful to many businesses wanting to generate word of mouth. But don't assume that networking is the only way to generate new business from word of mouth. As you will see, word-of-mouth marketing is much more than networking.

Word-of-mouth marketing is...

- the most natural way to promote your business.
- the lowest-cost promotion method you can find.
- the lowest-risk promotion method.
- the most powerful form of business development, harnessing the personal communication energy of dozens of people who speak on your behalf and who actually bring you new customers.
- an excellent way to motivate your employees and your customers.
- the most enjoyable, fulfilling form of marketing management.

- the promotional method most consistent with known consumer behaviors. People talk.
- one of the most efficient targeting methods.
- the type of promotion most business professionals hope for but few plan for.

Word-of-mouth marketing is a significant part of your business, but it is, of course, only one aspect of your operations. You will also need competent accounting or legal advice, which are beyond the scope of this book. In addition, personnel management, cash flow management, purchasing, distributor relationships and product development are a few examples of other areas you will also need to consider as you manage your business toward success.

So let your customers do the talking, and enjoy the sounds of success!

Chapter 1

*S*triking Gold Through Word-of-Mouth Marketing

*"*There is only one thing in the world worse than being talked about, and that is not being talked about.*"*

— *Oscar Wilde*

*"*To keep a customer demands as much skill as to win one.*"*

— *American proverb*

*7*he way the world does business is changing. International competition for lower prices and higher-quality products has sounded the wake-up call to business. Increased financial pressure from foreign competition is making industries find new ways to cut the cost of doing business. Add to this the belt-tightening business consolidations taking place in the face of the shrinking level of new markets and the maturing of most markets in developed countries.

To these pressures mix in the changes taking place in marketing. In many industries the dependence on paid advertising has been declining. No longer does mass media advertising enjoy the central role in marketing. Consumers are saturated with thousands of commercial messages daily. To curtail massive advertising budgets as well as find new ways to communicate with consumers, companies have turned to other methods, such as direct marketing and in-store promotions, to signal value.

Promotion is the part of the marketing mix that signals value to buyers before, during and after the sale. As you will see in this book, word of mouth is vital to the sale *before* a consumer makes the purchase. In fact, those who come to your business based on someone's recommendation come presold on the product. The astute business owner encourages word of mouth *during* the transaction and uses word-of-mouth tactics to encourage grapevine marketing *after* the sale.

Although word of mouth is to a great degree controlled by the satisfied customer, it is the face-to-face relationship that the customer has with someone else that is so powerful. Friends talk about things of mutual interest. And it is this mutuality that makes the communication relevant and credible for the one receiving the information. When friends converse, their defenses are down. This means they are more receptive to advice and will be more inclined to follow that advice because of the relationship. The messages don't get lost.

Word of mouth can help you achieve several purposes:

- Establish relationships with distributors
- Launch new products and new companies
- Break through cultural barriers
- Gather competitive intelligence
- Recruit employees, volunteers, members and donors

A wide range of industries survive and thrive based on its benefits, including:

- Manufacturers, distributors and retailers
- Sales companies and nonprofit organizations
- Product companies and service companies
- Political campaigns

As a method of communication, word of mouth serves the broadest range of industries. It is used in every culture of the world. And, though it is arguably the least costly form of promotion, it covers the largest proportion of the population when compared with any other single method of advertising. At certain moments on certain days, television and radio can reach hundreds of millions of people with a message. But word of mouth reaches billions of people *every day*.

Consumers—The Driving Force

The single most powerful driving force in the evolution of business is an ever-increasing number of sophisticated, informed consumers. Barraged with sales pitches and commercial messages, consumers are wary and skeptical. They are trying to cut through the hype to get to the essence of the promotional signals given them in advertisements. One of the best ways for them to accomplish this is by getting a recommendation from an experienced customer. Hungry for this information, many consumers actively seek it out.

Educated in the ways of the marketplace, a consumer is your advocate, not your enemy. An educated consumer has enormous influence upon others. Customers who are educated about your business are more likely to come to you to resolve a complaint, rather than spreading bad news. They are more likely to be satisfied with their purchases. Even if the information you give them is unrelated to your products, the process of education increases your positive contact with them.

The speed with which companies bring new products to market has been shortened from two or more years to six months, and in some cases just a few days. The result is a controlled chaos of competition for the mind of the consumer. Yet through all this competition, word of mouth consistently stands out as the most powerful method to signal value.

Business owners have tried many advertising tactics over the last few years, and sometimes with disappointing results. This experimentation has left some business owners skeptical about the value of marketing. I have heard business owners say, "You feel you must buy something, but it never works the way you expect." Small-business owners who have tried traditional promotional tactics are returning to the basics of word-of-mouth marketing, but many do not know how to take an organized approach to this challenge.

Negative Word of Mouth Happens More Than You Think

In some industries a high percentage of customers leave a business disappointed, disillusioned or dissatisfied, and decide not to return. Up to 95 percent of unhappy customers will not tell you that they are unhappy with the service they received; however, they *are* willing to tell someone else. In fact, marketing experts say that people who are unhappy with a business professional's service are ten times more likely to communicate their unhappiness to someone else than is someone who is happy with the service received.

Here is another shocking point: Up to 80 percent of lost clients can be attributed to a problem with the people who work at a business. It might be indifference, poor performance or just a lack of ability to get along with people.

Late at night in a desert town, a businessman driving from Ohio to California stopped to rest. He chose a well-known national motel chain, one that advertised the lowest price of any national chain. If he stayed in their motel, the radio spokesman promised, he could be assured of a good experience.

During the check-in process the motel clerk asked if he would be needing the telephone. He said yes and paid the $5 deposit. After getting settled in his room, he dialed and listened to six unanswered rings before hanging up. He repeated the process twice more at ten-minute intervals. Although he was frustrated at not being able to reach his party, he had no cause to blame the motel management. Not yet, anyway.

Eager to get on the road, he went to the office early in the morning to check out. Because he had not been successful in any of his three attempts on the telephone, he figured that he had his $5 telephone deposit waiting for him. Wrong. Instead he found a phone bill for $1.35 and a rude clerk. Here is the conversation that followed.

"I'm checking out of my room and have a $5 telephone deposit to pick up." He spoke through the double-thick glass window with the small opening at the bottom for passing money and motel keys. He wasn't sure the sleepy-looking clerk heard him, as it was the same clerk who had checked him in the evening before.

"Just a minute while I check the computer." She turned and went to a printer, pushed a few buttons, and they both watched as computer paper spurted from the inside of the printer case. She returned to the window bearing the news. "Says here you made three telephone calls, and that'll cost you $1.35. You get $3.65 in change." She pushed the computer paper and a pen through the small opening. "Sign here on this receipt."

"Excuse me, but I didn't make three telephone calls. I tried to make three calls but didn't succeed."

"Computer says you made three calls. Do you want your money or don't you? Sign here." She looked disgusted.

"But I'm telling you I didn't make three telephone calls. When I tried, I got no answer each time. Why have you charged me for calls I did not complete?"

"You'll have to take that up with the telephone company. I'm not giving you your money until you sign for it." Her jaw tightened.

"But I'm on the road traveling. How am I supposed to do that? I'd like to speak with the manager of the motel to see if we can resolve this."

"I am the manager," she said with a gruff voice.

"Then may I speak with the motel owner?"

She rolled her eyes in disgust. "Sure. You can contact them in _____." Heavy sigh.

"That's not going to help us get this resolved here right now, is it?" He was getting steamed, too.

"Listen, mister, do you want me to call the sheriff? Either you sign the paper for your refund or I'm calling the sheriff." She was actually shouting through the thick glass.

She had him there. He signed for the $3.65 and has been telling literally hundreds of people the story of the rude motel manager. He delights in naming the motel and its location.

That emotionally charged experience illustrates how much negative word of mouth can be generated from just one short conversation. The effects go far beyond a desert town. The businessman got a motel room at a low price. But that fact is little consolation for being treated rudely, and for being upset for the rest of the day.

The Positive Side of Word of Mouth

Contrast this story with an experience I had in Riverside, California. One morning I found that my car engine thermostat was stuck closed. When this happens, the coolant in the engine does not circulate, and the engine tends to overheat.

With a few tools in the trunk, I drove to the nearest Chief Auto Parts store to purchase the new thermostat. The store manager helped me look in the parts catalogue to locate the correct part. In a friendly voice he said, "If you run into any problems, let me know." I think he knew I was going to change the thermostat in his parking lot.

Forty-five minutes later, after several failed attempts to get the new thermostat seated and bolted in without any leaks, I took him up on his offer. Heavy black grease smeared on my hands and wrists, I stood in front of him with the sleeves of my white business shirt rolled up past the elbows.

"Did you remember to clean off the old gasket?"

"I tried, but I don't have a very good tool for that. I've been trying to scrape it with this screwdriver."

"Try again and then use this tube of sealant. If you still have trouble, let me know."

The next attempt worked like a charm. His tube of sealant, which I was happy to purchase, assured me that there would be no more leaks. Grateful for his help, I went in to thank him and to ask for a paper towel.

"It's my pleasure. I'll bet you're glad it doesn't leak now," he replied. "As for the towel, you can come in the back of the store and use our sink. Here is a tub of grease cleanser. You will have warm water and a couple of cloth towels to use."

That overwhelmed me. The warm water soothed my edgy nerves, and the fresh, clean towel felt great. After I washed my face and hands, I thanked him and walked out of the store determined to tell others about him and his store. I manage to work this story into most of my seminars on word-of-mouth marketing. By now I have used this event to illustrate to thousands of people how positive word of mouth gets started.

Word-of-Mouth Leverage

Up to 80 percent of people use recommendations from a family member, friend or business professional when making a purchase. Word of mouth is the primary way people get their information about products and services. Some rely on the word of just one person when making a decision. Think about the marketing potential this has for your business: What do you suppose your loyal customers say about *you?*

Each customer you have knows 200, 300 or even 400 other people. Each of these knows a few hundred more people. The potential total is one huge, interconnected grapevine. Closer to practical reality, however, there are probably three or four dozen people who know each of your customers well enough to speak with them often, and each of those people talks to three or four dozen others on a regular basis. That network can give you great marketing leverage. Some research has demonstrated that happy customers will tell as many as five or six prospective customers the good news about your business.

Add to this the scores of other people who overhear a happy client talking to a friend about your business. Even if they do not know your happy customer, they still stand there listening to him or her give a personal recommendation that will result in another new customer—either the listeners themselves or someone they tell. Think of the marketing power you can gain by tapping into this huge grapevine.

The power of word of mouth extends beyond this, however, because people with characteristics similar to those of your current clients know others with similar interests. People who are interested in investment talk with others who invest. People who want to buy a home talk with others who have just purchased one. People who are headed for divorce get advice from recent divorcees on which attorney to select. Neighbors talk with each other about which swimming pool contractors are reliable, which plumbers do quality work and which masonry contractors get the job done without prodding. People purchasing sports equipment talk with other sports enthusiasts. Dance students and their parents talk with others who have an interest in dance lessons. People talk over lunch about the good book they read or a movie they recently enjoyed. The list can go on and on.

Although most businesses believe in the power of word-of-mouth marketing, very few have developed word-of-mouth marketing plans. During consulting projects with new clients, I often ask why this is true. The most common answer is, "There's not a whole lot you can do about it. If it's going to happen, it just happens." Or I might hear, "The only thing I can do is treat my customers well and hope they make referrals." This book is written to overcome the misconception that nothing can be done to make word of mouth happen or that all you can do is treat your customers well. If you don't believe you can do anything about a problem, you are not likely to try. As you read this book, keep your mind open to this thought: You can do something to effect a positive word-of-mouth marketing program. You can enhance your reputation. You can see the results of happy clients talking and sending others to you.

Don't fool yourself into thinking that one method of advertising is responsible for sales volume. In reality, success results from a combination of signaling efforts—word of mouth being one of the most important. Like it or not, your customers talk about you and your products.

What They Are Talking About

Consumers talk about all kinds of things with one another. You may be surprised at what they say when they talk up your business to their friends. Here are the most common messages consumers send through the grapevine. The product or service they talk about

- provides needed information.
- respects them and their needs.
- offers practical solutions and benefits.
- is offered at a good price.
- is different from competing products and services.
- is friendly and helpful.

Generating positive word of mouth requires much more than a smile and a warm voice. When clients come to your business, their primary concern is that their purchase goal, their problem or their questions will be taken care of in a competent manner so that good results occur. When buying a tangible product, consumers want to know that that product will live up to and even exceed your claims.

Practical Strategies You Can Use Right Away

In this book I have collected a variety of practical ideas that business professionals have found successful. Some are simple to implement, requiring minimal staff training. Some are a little more involved and may require spending a small amount of money. They are your Action Agenda items designed to help you succeed in word of mouth.

Choose the Action Agenda ideas that best fit both your approach to running your business and your personality. If you stay with what you consider ethical, moral and professional, you will be true to yourself and enjoy your work more.

*A*ction *A*genda

1. *Reinforce the fact that you are competent.*   Whenever a new client comes to your business, someone in your company should make it a point to tell the person about pertinent past accomplishments, noting that you have

- successfully helped others with the same problem,
- had special training in the areas they need help with and
- taken a special interest in that subject.

A good way to communicate competence is to offer the client a brief example of how others faced this same situation and found a practical solution through your company.

2*. Refuse to be silent.*   Silence may be interpreted as incompetence. Give customers more information through personal conversations, written materials, conversations with their family members, telephone calls—every opportunity you can take. When you are silent they may develop anxiety. They may have unanswered questions. By contrast, if you discuss the aspects of their problem, how your solutions work, what to expect during follow-through and even some of the downside risks, you are more likely to have a happy client who will do anything for you, including referring others.

3*. Let the client know you are familiar with other elements that may have a direct bearing on their situation.*   Clients are amazed when you describe accurately what they are going through. They tend to believe your evaluation and accept your advice more quickly—and this both contributes to a positive outcome and builds your reputation.

4*. Involve the client in evaluating the solution.*   When you ask questions, make suggestions, describe similar problems, offer solutions and discuss implications, the client sees the logic of your evaluation and will leave with a heightened respect for your abilities.

5*. Reinforce the positive when clients are complimentary.*   When clients offer a statement about their level of happiness with you or the organization, acknowledge their appreciation.

6*. Seek out any negative feelings clients exhibit in your presence.*   Look for subtle nonverbal cues that the client is wondering about something, or is anxious, frustrated or having a negative experience. If you see a furrowed brow, ask the client directly. Such questions as "Is there something I need to know that you haven't told me?" and "You seem upset about something. Is it something I can help you with?" leave the door open for them to tell you what they are upset about.

7.   *Provide telephone staff with a prepared script to use when a prospective client calls.*   They should tell the client that you are "knowledgeable, interested, informative," etc., as well as any specific positive comments from other clients. Your staff should never be at a loss for words to describe you in terms that clients actually use in making a selection.

8.   *Open your mind to new ways to generate talk.*   As you read the examples in this book from other businesses, try to think of how to apply their methods to your own situation. Many ideas are directly transferable with only minor cosmetic changes.

9.   *Read the business journals and newspapers with an eye toward word-of-mouth marketing ideas.*   Embedded in feature stories about successful enterprises you will find tactical gems of word-of-mouth marketing wisdom. Become your own marketing expert by knowing who is doing what in word of mouth. When an article simply makes reference to the fact that the majority of a business's customers come through word of mouth, call the business and ask what they do to make that happen.

10.   *Do some networking to gather more ideas.*   At professional conventions, local business groups, chamber of commerce meetings and other settings where your peers gather, listen for examples of word-of-mouth tactics that others use. If you don't hear anything, ask a few simple questions to focus the conversation on word of mouth.

11.   *Survey customers' perceptions of your business and its strengths and weaknesses.*   You can give customers a brief questionnaire asking them to respond to the major quality or service issues central to your products and services (see Figure 1.1). Have respondents rate your performance on these quality or service attributes; the importance they give to each of the attributes; and their experience with other companies on these same attributes. You can refine the following list of commonly rated attributes to fit your company and industry.

Convenience	Durability	Reliability
Responsiveness	Competence	Style
Courtesy	Credibility	Quality of materials
Security	Safety	Accessibility
Usability	Knowledge	Understanding
Customization	Promptness	Visual appeal

12. ***Draw perceptual maps using the results of your survey.*** Using the average scores for each service attribute, plot the results of your survey on a "map" like the one in Figure 1.2 to determine

FIGURE 1.1 Sample Survey Questions To Use

---

1. Based on your experience with our company, how would you rate us for each of the following?

	Excellent	*Good*	*Fair*	*Poor*
Responsiveness	1	2	3	4
Competence	1	2	3	4

2. Based on your own experience with the types of services we provide, how important is each of the following to you personally?

	Very Important	*Somewhat Important*	*Not Very Important*	*Not at All Important*
Responsiveness	1	2	3	4
Competence	1	2	3	4

3. Based on what you know or what you have heard about other companies, how would you rate our competitors on the following points?

	Excellent	*Good*	*Fair*	*Poor*
Responsiveness	1	2	3	4
Competence	1	2	3	4

---

what consumers think of your company. One map can be created for any combination of two attributes. Show the charts to champion clients both to get their feedback and to educate them on the results. Ask for their opinions on how to improve your position on the map. Show charts of positive outcomes to prospective clients, to your employees and to key players in the industry infrastructure.

13. ***Find out what customers dislike and be different.*** Most industries have reports of market research showing the things that irritate customers. Read your industry trade journals and newsletters or talk to industry experts. Identify the top two or three consumer irritations, and then make your product or company so different that customers cannot possibly miss it. If the positive changes you make do not attract notice at first, keep working at it until your champion customers begin talking about them. If the difference is obvious, customers will talk up your business.

FIGURE 1.2   Sample Perceptual Map

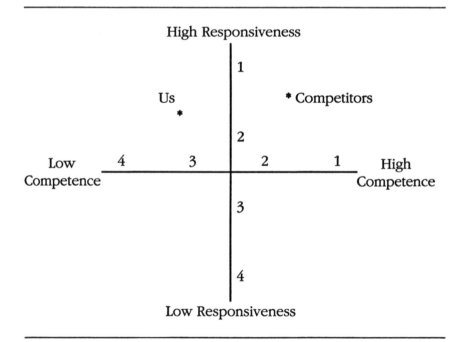

$\mathcal{P}$rofiles Of $\mathcal{S}$uccess

French Meadow Bakery
Minneapolis, Minnesota

Business Profile: French Meadow Bakery bakes and distributes nationally a line of fresh bread products sold in natural food retail stores, restaurants, airlines and institutions.

Word-of-Mouth Tactics: Lynn Gordon, company founder, has a very small advertising budget and has not hired a public relations firm. "My secret," says Lynn, "is that I am willing to devote all my time to the business. I don't buy things for the business unless I can afford them. I keep my own income low so I don't bleed the company of the cash it needs. I am a picky customer myself, and I focus on creating the highest-quality product; then I personally oversee the customer service."

Word of mouth started spreading almost immediately after the company got started. Lynn demonstrated her sourdough bread at one food show in Chicago. The professional chefs among the show participants started recommending her bread, leading to invitations to other shows. Based on the professional chefs' recommendations, a consumer magazine featured her products. This opened the door for national distribution through the natural-food merchandisers. Magazine and newspaper food writers began reporting on her bread products. "All this publicity started because of the quality of the product. People simply liked it, and they liked the way I took care of customers," says Gordon.

Lynn admits managing word of mouth by the seat-of-the-pants method. She sends thank-you notes to referral sources, personally handles customer service calls, listens and talks to customers, exhibits at trade shows and gives free samples to people who influence purchasing decisions.

Results: Word of mouth accounts for 50 percent of French Meadow Bakery's national sales and 90 percent of local sales. *(Used by permission from French Meadow Bakery)*

FIGURE 1.3 Word-of-Mouth Marketing Assessment

Before reading the rest of the book, take a few minutes to honestly evaluate how well your company lets customers do the talking. Then begin thinking about how you can improve your word-of-mouth marketing efforts.

Instructions: The statements below describe some businesses. Use the following scale to determine how true each statement is for your business. Write a number on each blank line.

1 = Very true
2 = Somewhat true
3 = Not applicable
4 = Somewhat untrue
5 = Very untrue

_____ You have no formal, ongoing information-gathering process to determine specific areas of your service that need improvement.

_____ You do not get specific suggestions or complaints from clients on a regular basis.

_____ Some of your employees consider troublesome clients as pests or problems to get rid of.

_____ Your business contact with clients is confusing.

_____ Your business procedures lack coordination.

_____ Clients who refer business to you do not receive appreciation on a regular basis.

_____ You do not know who your referring clients are.

_____ Problem solving for clients is laborious and difficult.

_____ Someone at your business undermines positive word of mouth through indifference or attitude.

_____ The owner is not involved in promoting positive word of mouth.

_____ You get very few referrals from word of mouth.

_____ Your business policies frustrate or anger your clients.

FIGURE 1.3 Word-of-Mouth Marketing Assessment, *continued*

_____ You have no formal plan to build referrals.

_____ You don't know who is talking about you to others.

_____ You make no attempt to combine word of mouth with other advertising methods.

_____ **TOTAL**

Score Interpretation

15–25 Your business is not doing much to build word of mouth.

26–35 Your business considers word of mouth secondary to other things.

36–48 Your business is about average in implementing a word-of-mouth program.

49–60 With a few improvements, your business will have a strong word-of-mouth program.

61–75 Your word-of-mouth program is probably better than most.

Chapter 2

*W*hat It Takes To Succeed

"Goodwill is the only asset that competition cannot undersell or destroy."

— Marshall Field

*I*f I can boil down an idea to just one or two elements, I will be able to remember it. So I've boiled down word-of-mouth marketing to two basic issues: stopping negative word of mouth as much as possible, and following a consistent program to promote positive word of mouth.

As simple as this sounds, there is a significant amount of effort that must be put into a marketing program to help it succeed. Talking about saving money and business development won't help if you don't follow your word-of-mouth marketing program carefully. Positive word-of-mouth marketing does not happen by itself. It happens because of specific skills that are consistently applied in the normal working environment with each customer.

The Threshold of Excellent Service

Most clients will not say a word about you, either positive or negative, if their experience is merely adequate. If you simply meet their basic expectations, they will have nothing to shout about to their friends. However, if you exceed customers' expectations, they will find that remarkable.

For each client there is a threshold of service excellence (the place where you exceed the client's expectations) that must be crossed before positive word of mouth takes place. The challenge is to find this threshold during every telephone call and every encounter before, during and after the sale. The challenge never goes away, but it may change with changing times and changing consumer needs.

As they experience excellent service, satisfied clients will gradually want more and more (it's human nature). But if they keep coming back to you and then keep talking about it to their friends, doesn't that make your extra effort worth it? Does it matter if other people find out how well your clients are treated? Won't they get jealous and want to buy your products, too? Yes. That's the whole idea of word-of-mouth marketing: building the business with happy consumers who talk about it to others. Of course, there may be limits to what you can do for clients. You have only so many hours and dollars to spend each day. Most reasonable people understand that you cannot give them the moon for a penny.

Finding the Threshold

Your search for the threshold of excellent service can get frustrating without a few guidelines, so let me suggest six fertile areas. First, think in terms of the existing relationships between your company and its customers. Is the relationship positive with each person the customer contacts in your company? Being friendly is necessary, but friendliness alone does not constitute excellent service. People skills require that employees be well trained in their jobs, confident, communicative, reliable, courteous, credible, energetic, knowledgeable, attentive and caring, with an attitude of "I can do it for you now."

These positive people skills communicate to clients that you do care, are there for them and know what you are doing. If you are willing to become obsessed with positive word-of-mouth marketing, you will never be satisfied with the level of excellence in your service. You will constantly seek to improve, knowing that you can make a difference in your customers' lives.

Look at the people skills that promote positive word of mouth and reward them in your business. Don't be afraid to identify the attributes that cause negative word of mouth among clients.

The second place to look for the threshold of excellence is in the systems (your company procedures, policies, production methods, environment, etc.) that are in place for serving customers from the moment they call with an inquiry about your products to the time when they no longer need your product or service. Here the key ingredients are responsiveness, efficiency, flexibility, consistency, durability, convenience, uncomplicated procedures, reliability, accessibility and security. To assess the responsiveness of your systems, consider the following questions:

1. Are your hours of business flexible to meet the needs of working clients?
2. Do you handle clients' finances the same way each time they visit?
3. Do you follow through on your commitments to customers?
4. Does the product work as the consumer expects?
5. Does the product resist damage or decay?
6. Does the product perform well under the most demanding of circumstances?
7. Is the product safe?

The third place to find access to excellence is in a product's remarkable qualities. Remarkable qualities are sometimes tangible features. However, most often what is remarkable is the intangible cluster of benefits that buyers or users get from the product. What sets your product apart is its remarkable ability to assist buyers in solving problems or achieving personal or organizational objectives.

The fourth area for crossing the threshold of excellence is in pricing. Word of mouth spreads fast when consumers perceive great value for their money. If value is not readily seen, you can help the consumer by explaining the source of value from his or her point of view.

A fifth way to the excellence threshold is through accessibility. People talk about how accessible your product or service is. Your loyal customers will recommend your product to others if it is accessible. They will give specific instructions on how, where and when to buy your product.

The sixth road to excellence is in the promotion tactics you use. Consumers rely on the word of someone else to a great degree when making product selections. Often it is word of mouth that alerts them to paid advertising. Bombarded with thousands of advertising messages, consumers learn to hear what they need to hear, and word of mouth guides them in listening.

The opposite is also true. Paid advertising can guide a consumer in listening to word-of-mouth recommendations. Paid advertising, point-of-purchase promotion and direct sales give consumers ideas of what to ask their friends and families when they consider your product. Also, consumers look for consistency and congruence between paid advertising and the word-of-mouth messages they get from others. When consistency is lacking, consumers tend to believe the word of someone who is experienced with the product.

These areas make up the most important qualities of the threshold of perceived value in any business. Slip-ups in any of them can result in unhappy clients and negative word of mouth. Exceeding expectations here can result in clients with positive things to say about you.

*A*ction *A*genda

14. *As the boss, put your mouth where your money is.* Unless you are willing to employ positive word-of-mouth marketing principles, your employees will not follow. Become a proponent for word of mouth in your office. Become possessed by it. Practice it. Talk about it. You may find that some employees have a greater commitment to promoting word of mouth than you do. If they perceive that you are less interested in promoting a consistent word-of-mouth program, they will get discouraged and their own commitment will gradually cool.

Evaluate how much time you actually devote to explaining or promoting word of mouth within the company. If you find that you *think* more about it than actually *talk* about it to employees and champion consumers, your program is still in your head and not yet a reality. When you begin making word of mouth a reality in your own work, you will expect employees to do the same. If, however, you mention your ideas a few times and then retreat to the safety of your office, your employees will get the message: The boss is really not serious about this word-of-mouth stuff.

15. *Train, train, train.*   We are never finished with word-of-mouth marketing. The company environment constantly changes and client needs change, too. Employees forget the importance of people skills over time. Or they leave and new employees come who have not been trained in your system of service. Set a consistent course of training and retraining until every employee improves his or her client relations skill to the level you desire. Expect the best and help employees achieve it.

16. *Segment the market.*   I'll say more about this later, but begin thinking now about how you can group your customers into meaningful categories for word-of-mouth marketing—for example, champion clients who speak about you often and swear by your company; new clients who need an exceptionally positive experience the first time they transact business with you (good impressions are made here); quiet clients; and clients in the larger middle group who are just waiting to be convinced.

17. *Remove the barriers to positive word of mouth.*   If you have several specialized jobs that involve a high degree of contact with customers, implement some cross-training to help your employees assist one another when necessary. Eliminate coordination barriers between technicians and receptionist and between supervisors and senior partners.

18. *Review company policies that exist for your convenience.* Change the ones you can to help put the client in control. Inform employees of the reasons behind the changes.

19. *Combat the indifference of unmotivated employees.*   Help them see the importance of positive word of mouth. Give them the power to make decisions and take actions for clients when problems arise.

20. *Use staff meetings to conduct creative problem-solving sessions.*   Analyze specific consumer complaints. Look ahead for potential problems before they become a source of irritation to clients.

21. *Give champion clients more information to tell others.* You will read more about champion clients later in the book. For now, begin thinking about how you can keep customers informed about what is going on behind the scenes in the business. What type of information would you want to know if you were a client?

22. *Give customers a direct, personal experience with your business.* In an attempt to maintain professionalism, employees can seem more interested in the company policies or even the details of work than in the client. Except for the mandatory words, looks and gestures, some customers feel like they are ignored. To prevent this, make sure someone says something personal to the client. Use the customer's name more than once. If you don't know his or her name, find out and then use it. Ask a question that engages clients in conversation. Look them in the eye and speak directly to them. As obvious as this sounds, it doesn't happen in many businesses.

23. *Give customers opportunities to tell others.* You're not out to manipulate consumers' behavior. What you want is to help them do what they naturally enjoy doing on their own: talking about you if they believe you have a quality product. By giving them things to talk about to their friends and neighbors, you give them an opportunity to fulfill an important role in their social network. Just think how difficult it is to keep a secret. That's why marketing through the grapevine is so powerful: Almost nothing can stop it once it gets started.

24. *Show your appreciation when they refer people.* Genuine appreciation is always welcome, and you can't go wrong by expressing your gratitude every time a satisfied customer refers someone to you. When thanking them, say, "Our reputation is the most valuable thing we have in this community. We know you play a part in sharing that reputation with others, and we want you to know how much we appreciate you." The best way to do this is face to face. Place a stick-on note on your desk or at the register to remind you about that champion customer's hard work so that the next time he or she comes in, you can tell the customer how much you appreciate what he or she has done for you. If you see this person infrequently, write a short thank-you note and also thank him or her on the telephone. Even if you send a note or call, however, be sure to thank the client personally when you see him or her the next time.

25. *Keep track of your champions.*   Start by making a list of the people who have referred others to you. Read that list to employees and create a plan of action to develop a personal relationship with those people. This in itself will exceed the threshold of their positive expectations.

Don't be put off if, at your first meeting with a prospective champion, you get a cool reception. If you work in a large business with a high volume of clients, remember that three or four of every ten clients may be champions. Getting to know who they are is step one. Maintaining a positive personal relationship is step two.

If you need to divide up the list, get several people in your business involved in keeping track of champions. Think of it this way: If all other forms of promotion were taken away except word-of-mouth marketing, how closely would you maintain contact with your champions? These relationships with the people who speak for you in the community would become critical to you, and you would do just about anything ethical and legal to maintain your good reputation and their good favor.

26. *Start small and stay focused.*   When you initiate a word-of-mouth marketing program, begin with the basic elements and then embellish the program as needed. Follow these steps as a guide.

Identification — Identify by name the clients and other people who are responsible for your good reputation; make and keep current a written list. This is your bank account of good will. Manage it wisely and you will receive bountiful dividends to your marketing investment. Identification also involves diagnosing your business to find the areas in your products and services that need improvement. Start (or continue) your never-ending search for high quality today.

Encouragement — Pick one or two ideas you can implement consistently that will promote your reputation and get clients to continue talking for you. There are more ideas in this book than one company can implement consistently. Select a few that you can follow through on and stick with it. Encouragement also means finding ways to encourage other people in your business to support a positive word-of-mouth program. And it means asking in a tasteful manner for referrals.

Gratitude — Select one or two methods of showing gratitude when your loyal supporters refer others to your business. You cannot say thank you in a genuine manner too many times. Gratitude breeds gratitude and results in your customers talking about you to their friends and family.

27. *Don't advertise your product or service's excellence until you know it's true.* Nothing is gained by raising consumer expectations past the point at which you can deliver. If you roll out the hype before your company is ready, you will be setting yourself up for negative word of mouth. It is much better to develop the internal infrastructure for excellence *before* you advertise. I'm not saying that you should stop all advertising until you have your store in order; just don't promise something you can't deliver. Promising that you are "the dealer that cares" when a few key employees treat customers like they are a pain in the neck will undermine your credibility and create consumer frustration.

28. *Develop a vision statement for your company that incorporates word of mouth.* Vision statements are usually brief descriptions of where the organization wants to be in the future. It should mention the position your organization will have in the minds of key consumers. In your vision statement, try to set your organization apart from competitors. Following are examples of vision statements drawn from two different industries:

"Our pizza and pasta restaurant will be known in our community through what our customers say about our attractive atmosphere and our generous serving sizes."

"Our auto service company will be known as the place to come for solutions to the most difficult repair problems."

29. *Set objectives that challenge your organization.* Objectives can focus on just about any perspective you wish. For example, you may want to emphasize slow, consistent growth. If so, set a growth rate objective of 1 percent per month. It doesn't sound like much, but it adds up to 12 percent growth per year. Another emphasis can be on the champions. For example, your objective may be to identify, encourage and reward at least ten new champions each month. Be creative. Here are some other examples:

- Increase the number of thank-you notes sent out to champions each month by 10 percent.
- Increase the overall percent of new customers patronizing your organization based on word of mouth by 5 percent.
- Increase to 90 percent the proportion of employees who are active participants in your word-of-mouth marketing efforts.

There are four traditional rules for setting business objectives. First, objectives should be specific rather than general. Establish target numbers to shoot for. Second, select objectives that can be monitored and measured during the normal course of doing business. Without a tracking method in place, you will find it difficult to know how well you are doing, and your employees will lose interest. Third, word-of-mouth marketing objectives should be challenging. Setting your sights high creates a sense of urgency. When employees participate in setting objectives, don't be surprised if they set them higher than you would if you were setting them yourself. Last, do your best to make your objectives attainable. Learning how to do this requires a broad knowledge of your business and of the marketing environment in which you work.

30. *Establish a team of employees to lead the others in word-of-mouth marketing.* An exciting way to accomplish this is to set up a self-directed work team to which you act as coach. Under this approach, team members are involved with the core of your company's vision. They have higher energy and more commitment to succeed. Your word-of-mouth marketing team should include individuals from a variety of perspectives, such as finance, operations, production, customer service, delivery and sales. The following are ground rules for setting up and coaching such a team:

- Give the team an actual assignment to set up the word-of-mouth marketing function.
- Give team members extra training in word-of-mouth marketing principles and in self-directed work teams.
- Give the team the authority to make plans, implement work tactics and control word-of-mouth marketing activities.

- Place clearly defined limits on responsibilities for influencing operations and on how much may be spent for word of mouth.
- Recognize that these directions and limits may be adjusted as the team matures and succeeds.
- Remember that you, as coach, are responsible for results of the team's work.
- Require that the team rotate the responsibilities of team leadership among the group members.
- Establish clear rules for adding or deleting individuals from participation on the team.
- Have the team report to you within 24 hours of each team meeting, giving you a summary of what was discussed and what actions they are taking to move forward.
- Recognize that team dynamics change over time. Members' early excitement will change to frustration a few months later. If they are persistent, the frustration will give way to mature problem solving and eventual success.
- Allow enough time for your team to get through the difficult stages of development.
- Remember that you are the coach, not the team leader.
- Read two or three good books on self-directed work teams.

31. *Begin a formal "company eavesdropping" program.*   Let your employees know that you or the word-of-mouth marketing team will be listening for interactions that cause frustration, anxiety, anger, disappointment and irritation among your customers.

32. *Conduct a S.W.O.T. analysis of your reputation.* A S.W.O.T. analysis weighs the **S**trengths, **W**eaknesses, **O**pportunities and **T**hreats of your business. Strengths are internal resources and capabilities that assist your company in fulfilling its goals. Weaknesses are internal problems or lack of capabilities that detract from goal achievement. Opportunities and threats are external dynamics of the market that affect your success. When conducting a S.W.O.T. analysis, it pays to be realistic. If you think you are too close to your own business to be honest, ask someone who has no stake in your success or failure to help you with this process. Use the following list as a guide.

Strengths	Weaknesses	Opportunities	Threats
_____	_____	_____	_____
_____	_____	_____	_____
_____	_____	_____	_____

33. *Evaluate the leverage your reputation gives you.* Your company brings many resources to the table of business success. Among all these, how much influence does your reputation have? Use the following checklist to assign a weight to your reputation compared with the other resources at your disposal. For each item listed below, place a percentage of influence next to the word. When you have finished assigning values to all the items, the total should be 100 percent. Cross out any items that do not apply to your business.

Market share	_____
Product quality	_____
Strength of distribution system	_____
Sales force effectiveness	_____
Production efficiency	_____
Management performance	_____
Cash flow strength	_____
Ability of work force	_____
Technology/technical skill	_____
Relationships with suppliers	_____
Service quality	_____
Advertising and publicity effectiveness	_____
Reputation	_____
TOTAL	_____ 100 %

34. ***Deal with customers in a consistent manner.*** Consistency establishes realistic expectations and reinforces the customer's memory, binding the things he or she thinks about (seasons, events in their lives, etc.) to your company. When you are consistent with your loyal customers, they are confident that what they say about you remains accurate over time. Then, when the champion customer gets positive feedback that a friend's experience with your company was equivalent to his or her own, this reinforces the value of making more referrals to your company. When you are consistent, your loyal customers are more likely to seek more information from you to pass on to others. In terms of word of mouth, consistency is important in the quality of products and services you provide. It is also important for special promotional events. If you always have a special promotion in July, your customers will come to expect this and will tell their friends in advance. If you have a special event without fail every February, your champion customers will help you communicate this fact to others. If you are inconsistent in when and what promotions you offer, however, your loyal customers will be confused and thus will hesitate to tell others.

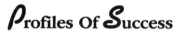

*P*rofiles Of *S*uccess

Anderson Landscaping
Lancaster, Massachusetts

Business Profile: Landscape construction company serving the high-end residential market.

Word-of-Mouth Tactics: When the high-end residential customer obtains competing bids, it is often a recommendation from someone else that makes the difference regardless of price. "This type of consumer depends on personal relationships to get information about who can be trusted," says Fred Anderson, founder and owner of Anderson Landscaping. "Their budget is bigger, but their expectations are higher. They are thoroughly involved with the landscape purchase."

The company gets referrals for some of the most sought-after landscape construction jobs in eastern Massachusetts by maintaining responsive relationships with his clients and with other professionals who serve the target market he prefers. Satisfied customers, landscape architects, general contractors, suppliers of custom products and even other landscape companies all refer business to Anderson. Fred is constantly educating them about how landscaping is done, the wide range of materials involved and the quality of his work. One of the tools he uses is a color portfolio showing dramatic before-and-after pictures of how he completely transformed a client's property.

Fred emphasizes detail-oriented precision in every element of his work. This precision is evident in the design and estimating part of the process as well as in the installation of materials. "When we work on a project that is costing the homeowner $150,000 just for landscaping, we cannot afford to make an estimation or installation error," he says. "Professionals who recommend us to their customers are putting their own reputations on the line for us. We make sure trees, grass and other plants grow as expected. We also teach homeowners how to properly care for their new products so they can preserve and enjoy their investment."

Every referral results in a personal, formal acknowledgment from Fred Anderson. He has business cards and a trifold brochure with color photos of his work and testimonials from high-visibility clients. Every customer receives a few business cards to give to friends. Referring professionals receive extra attention from Fred. He routinely does small favors for both homeowners and referring professionals to let them know how much he appreciates their support.

Results: One hundred percent of new customers come by referral.
(Used by permission from Anderson Landscaping)

Chapter 3

*H*ow To Make the Grapevine Work for You

"He who does not know the force of words cannot know men."

— *Confucius*

"A thousand words will not leave so deep an impression as one deed."

— *Henrik Ibsen*

*S*cientists simply don't know some things about word-of-mouth marketing. It just works. Most marketing experts I know believe that word of mouth is by far the most effective way to communicate with consumers. That's why it is often called the best advertising in the world.

Other than direct contact, word of mouth from a happy client is the most personal and, therefore, the most powerful form of communication. It is powerful because a real person carries a message about you. This person is knowledgeable about your company. The message he or she gives to others is tailor-made to their interests. Further, this person is usually able to expound on your virtues with ease.

If you want a constant reminder of the most basic principles of word-of-mouth marketing, hang a sign on your wall containing two simple words that summarize everything: PEOPLE TALK.

How To Find the Talkers

We all talk, but social scientists know that some people get listened to more than others. Who gets listened to in your business? Here are the most important identifying characteristics. People who talk for you

- have already referred other customers to you (this is the most important indicator).
- are your most loyal customers.
- are naturally outgoing and sociable.
- have recent experience with your company.
- have a lot of detailed information about your business and the people who work there.
- have a natural enthusiasm when speaking.
- speak convincingly.
- are in positions of leadership in a family, company, club or community (they didn't get in these positions without people listening to them).
- are socially mobile—in other words, they get around.
- read magazines or other materials dealing with products of interest or dealing with the marketplace in general.
- exhibit a high degree of interest in a product or service in the same or a related category.
- show personal interest in your business through questions and comments.
- have demonstrated personal gratitude for your excellent service, calling on the telephone to tell you, writing a thank-you note or saying something directly to you.
- tell you that others turn to them for help in difficult situations.
- say that they read a lot of advertising, search for coupons, and try to keep up on the latest and the best deals in the marketplace.
- tell you that they are active in local, regional or national politics.

You may not be able to apply all these factors equally to all customers, but use your best judgment and identify *by name* those who are the most likely candidates. Have your associates or employees help by making a list of people to whom others listen. Don't think about long-term customers only; your best promoters can be new clients. What you are looking for is leadership—those to whom others listen.

Four Types of Market Leaders

Four categories of people constitute your reputation builders: opinion leaders, marketing mavens, influentials and product enthusiasts.

Opinion leaders are people whose opinions are widely respected within social groups. These are the trend-setters who influence others by purchasing new products early. Some opinion leaders can be categorized as product enthusiasts (see below). They watch the development of certain products with interest and stay current on the latest versions of products. These people can be active purchasers themselves or simply industry watchers who review (even in the press) new products. Opinion leaders get their information from (and spread their influence primarily because of) their firsthand experience with products and services within specific categories. For example, interest in the personal computer was influenced initially by people who toyed with computers as a hobby. These individuals read magazines, watched news reports, attended conventions and generally kept themselves informed about developments in the personal computer industry. Others turned to them for advice because they were knowledgeable.

Opinion leaders (also called tastemakers, change agents, fashion leaders and high mobiles) may be perceived as mavericks by members of their interest group. Yet they have high self-confidence and low social anxiety about being different, because they believe that their difference is related to the direction in which the group is moving. These individuals think of themselves as giving information to others.

Some opinion leaders have interests in more than one area and contact with more than one social network. Consequently, they are exposed to more innovations than the general population. They can also be market mavens, influentials and product enthusiasts. What matters is that they have influence over the purchasing patterns of others.

Marketing mavens are people who make it their business to know, in general, where to get the best deals in the marketplace. Their specialty is not necessarily a single product category or two, but rather where to get value for your money. They may or may not also be an opinion leader (i.e., focus on specific product categories), but they are involved in a general way with purchasing experiences. They stay in touch with what is available and where to get the best prices for many kinds of products. They know where to shop. They read magazines like *Consumer Reports*, read local shopper's guides, collect or read coupons, pay attention to a wide variety of advertising messages, talk with other marketing mavens and opinion leaders, and engage in window shopping.

Marketing mavens have a high degree of social interaction with others on subjects relating to shopping in general. People depend on them for current information, and some develop a sense of obligation to keep current on behalf of the information seekers who check with them. They anticipate speaking with family or friends about shopping, so they hunt for the best information to give when asked.

Influentials are known as social activists—politically involved advisers for the rest of society. This small group, making up about 12 percent of the population, reads magazines like *The Atlantic Monthly, Harpers, The New Republic, The New Yorker, National Review* and others covering the wide spectrum of political ideas. They have wide-ranging interests and consume large quantities of printed information about a variety of issues affecting society in general, including marketplace information. You may find influentials who know the inside scoop in your industry, such as how profits are made, the contributing factors to current competition, distribution channel dynamics, or the political forces internal and external to your industry.

Influentials enjoy knowing what is going on and why. They attend public meetings and communicate with local, regional or national legislators. Influentials are more likely to hold elected or appointed offices in organizations. While they are found in every class in society, influentials are probably slightly better educated than others in their social class. They tend to be risk-takers as consumers, trying new products sooner than the rest of the public. Finally, influentials are well connected in the local economy. You can depend on them to know many other influentials, opinion leaders and highly visible people.

Product enthusiasts are the people who sustain a long-term interest in a product or category of products. Wine connoisseurs, computer wizards, sports car buffs and audiophiles are examples of common product enthusiasts in American culture. Compared with the product enthusiast, some other consumers don't care very much about the products they buy as long as those products perform. Product enthusiasts maintain a constant vigilance and sensitivity for product-related information that they may come across accidentally. Enthusiasts are on a constant search for more and especially up-to-date information. They subscribe to special-interest magazines, browse in specialty stores that carry the products that interest them, and spend time talking with others about the product or its use.

As product enthusiasts continue their quest for knowledge and experience with a product, they become experts. This expertise helps them select products. It gives them an edge in negotiating in the marketplace and it increases their influence over other consumers.

(Note: For the sake of simplicity, I most often use the term *opinion leaders* or *champion customers,* because the four categories described above hold this in common: They influence others' purchasing habits. However, when considering a word-of-mouth marketing tactic for one group, try to make the application for other groups as well.)

How Champion Customers Create Success

Opinion leaders help your business succeed by

- giving helpful, realistic information to their listeners.
- reducing the time others need to spend searching for information about a reputable company.
- reducing the perceived risk of trying your product.
- shaping the attitudes of prospective customers just before they make the decision whether to purchase.
- giving others inside information that is not accessible anywhere else.
- giving specific answers to questions that other customers cannot get anywhere else.
- correcting misunderstandings immediately.
- being a living example of a successful purchase experience.
- analyzing the nuances of others' concerns.
- confirming the truth or error of your paid advertising messages.
- giving messages that will be remembered amid all the clutter of advertising.
- providing an understanding of your company that can be gained no other way.
- informing others of what to expect during the purchase process.
- giving hints on how to make maximum use of the purchase relationship ("If you do such-and-such, you will get a better deal...").
- showing the prospect how to capitalize on your strengths and minimize the effects of your weaknesses.
- helping prospective clients get the most value for their money.

- helping others save money.
- improving the reliability of the information you transmit, thus reducing the risk, and associated costs, of inappropriate consumer expectations.
- putting their own reputations on the line for you.
- placing at your disposal their social connections with significant groups that look to them as leaders.

Why Champions Talk About You

Champion customers don't expect money for bringing in new clients. If you follow through carefully with them, they expect nothing more than a sincere thank you. So why do they bother to talk about your business? What's in it for them?

First, opinion leaders get an enormous amount of personal satisfaction from being listened to and looked up to. They enjoy being a point of reference for others. It helps them gain attention, enhances their status, helps them assert their superiority, and demonstrates their awareness and expertise. In the process, their credibility is reinforced.

Second, these champions usually get involved with your business. They like to get inside information, and they take their experience with you seriously. When asked about your products and services, they can't help themselves: They have to talk.

Third, talking about your business is a way they can enjoy social interaction with others.

Fourth, people talk about their purchase experiences to mentally process their own postpurchase anxieties ("Did I do the right thing?"). By talking to prospective clients, they get the results of their decisions out in the open to examine. They explore the benefits and risks of their own actions. Verbalizing the good experience they had with your company reinforces the feeling that, yes, they did the right thing.

Last, opinion leaders talk to help others. It gives them a sense of satisfaction if they can help someone else achieve a positive benefit they already enjoy.

Why Do Followers Listen?

Between 20 and 40 percent of the population can be considered opinion leaders in the broadest sense of the term. This means that the rest of the population either follows their advice or is staunchly independent and follows its own course. Why do so many follow?

Deciding on a product can be either a simple or a complex process. As the complexity of the purchase decision or their interest in your product increases, so does the likelihood that people will seek information from someone who knows you—someone with personal experience. When that happens, the chances are excellent that they will follow the advice they receive.

It is difficult to "test drive" an experience with a new company. Customers need the trusted recommendation of a friend or associate to help them. There's nothing wrong with depending on others for information and advice; it's part of our culture. We are all dependent some of the time for some products.

Followers are more likely to listen to opinion leaders if those leaders are perceived as being similar to themselves or to other members in their group. If information seekers believe that the opinion leader is slightly above them in status, all the better. Opinion leaders did not get to that position immediately. It took time for their followers to grant them the leadership position. With this history of respect and the opinion leader's own reputation as the background, followers take leaders' messages seriously.

When Does Your Reputation Spread?

First, business champions are just like everyone else: They talk in typical social situations. You know how conversations go—someone begins with one topic, and after a few minutes someone mentions another topic related to the first. I call this phenomenon *conversation swing*. When the topic of conversation naturally swings toward your category of product, an opinion leader client will think of you. It's human nature.

Second, they talk to other people in church, in a club, at work, in the neighborhood and in a recreation group. Most often, they talk to their families. Opinion leaders may be the most honest about what they experienced in your business when they are alone with their family. And their family members talk to their friends, associates, club members and other family members.

Third, opinion leaders speak about their positive purchase experiences soon after the transaction is completed—generally within 14 days. This is when the results of their actions are at the top of their minds. If the purchase required high involvement on their part, they think about it for longer than two weeks. During this critical time, they are more likely to bring up the subject with others.

Fourth, champion customers are ready at a moment's notice to speak about you with ease when they are asked a question. They give their own "agenda" first, thinking of the benefits and the features that stand out in their mind. They get immediate feedback—and if clarification is needed, they give it immediately.

Fifth, champions spread a positive message about you through nonverbal communications. This happens most often with immediate family members who have close contact with champion clients before, during and immediately after a purchase experience. Their reactions to how they were treated and their emotional states indicate their opinion of your service. Their feelings rise to the surface as soon as they get near people they trust.

Two Kinds of Grapevines

Word of mouth spreads both through close friendships and through casual acquaintances. Close friendships are important in word of mouth, because these people know the most about you and your product and can speak with the most authority. Strengthening these relationships will increase the *frequency* with which word of mouth spreads.

Casual acquaintances are important because they provide a critical link with other groups of close friends. Strengthening these relationships will increase the *reach* of your word-of-mouth efforts.

Controlled Chaos

Is it possible to predict the direction in which word of mouth will travel? Can you calculate the volume of messages that are transmitted by word of mouth within any given group?

Determining which groups receive word-of-mouth messages may seem to the casual observer to be unpredictable and prone to chance. The size and makeup of groups that accept the message of champions also appear at first glance to be controlled more by chance than predictable laws of human nature. But scientists have discovered that many things we think of as chance happenings are really events occurring at a different level of ordered complexity. This new science of chaos leads to the following five hypotheses:

1. Word of mouth is a phenomenon whose seemingly irregular patterns can be explained by the science of chaos.
2. Word-of-mouth events do not occur in a linear fashion—that is, one event occurring in an orderly sequence after just one other event. Instead, word-of-mouth dynamics occur in clusters of events.
3. Word-of-mouth growth is irregular in its expansion, with links through both close relationships and casual acquaintances occurring simultaneously.
4. Long-term effects of word of mouth may be highly sensitive to the initial conditions under which it starts. In other words, first impressions last and tend to repeat themselves under new circumstances.
5. What happens on a micro level (for example, one champion telling just one other person) is replicated on the large scale (larger numbers of customers telling the same story to groups).

Your Constant Opportunity To Build Business

Word-of-mouth marketing is an informal communication process in which the one making the recommendation is not speaking professionally on your behalf. These opinion leaders are highly persuasive, because they are perceived as having nothing to gain from their positive words. Word-of-mouth marketing is usually a face-to-face communication event, the most powerful form of communication. If you want a business that is based 80 to 90 percent on referrals, you will do what successful businesses have been doing for years: Follow these marketing tactics. Unlike traditional direct mail marketing, where you simply send a message uninvited to someone's home, word-of-mouth marketing is highly personal, although it demands constant effort to make it work. Word-of-mouth marketing is never done. You cannot simply assign it to an outside marketing consultant. It is a constant, unrelenting opportunity to build a business.

One business leader I spoke with said he believed that the word-of-mouth marketing ideas I had been gathering over the years should be applied to all customers, not just opinion leaders. "We should be giving all our customers the same level of attention that you suggest we give to opinion leaders," he said. To his surprise, I agreed.

*A*ction *A*genda

35. *List your champions for all employees to see.* Have an employee staff meeting to read the list and discuss it internally. Everyone should know how important these champions are for word-of-mouth marketing. Have the list available for quick reference and easy editing when a new talker surfaces. If your information system is computerized, make a note or put a flag next to each client who is identified as a talker. When these clients come into your business again, you will know them and overwhelm them with excellent service. If necessary, make four lists—one for each type of champion: opinion leaders, marketing mavens, influentials and product enthusiasts. Remember, there may be some overlap on the lists, as one person can fit in any of the four categories.

36. *Identify opinion leaders who are not your clients but who know you or know about you and can talk to others.* If you take word-of-mouth marketing seriously, you will want to know these people by name. You will know the professionals in the same building or down the block, the pharmacist, the shoe repairer, the clerk in the dress shop and anyone else who is an opinion leader in the community. Make a list of these people and begin planning specific activities to generate enthusiasm in their talk about you. Drop in to say hello when you go out for lunch; better yet, invite them to lunch. Let them have a few coupons for the free or discounted services you give only to opinion leader clients. These people can pass the positive word along just as well as clients can. Invite them in for a tour of your business and introduce them to the staff. Celebrate when they come in, and then send a personal thank-you note in appreciation for their time and support.

37. *Give more information to your opinion leaders about the business and its personnel.* If you need to, make a master checklist of the types of information you want all your champions to know. Each time an opinion leader comes in for visit, make sure to share more information. This not only is interesting to them, it also gives them something else to talk about when they leave the office. If you were mentioned in the news recently, give them a copy of the news clipping. If someone in your company gets an award from their peers, mention it. If someone gets married, mention it. Post resumes of senior partners or key personnel for customers to see.

38. *Identify the reputation builders.* Ask your clients what similar products or services they are interested in and give them more information about these, too. If they are interested in home water treatments, they are likely to talk about this (and about you) with their friends. If they watch television programs on the local cable television station, make sure to stock current copies of a program guide listing their favorite shows. Create a short checklist of items you can give to champions, and have a stock of magazine article reprints to hand out or some verbal information to give on those articles.

Product manufacturers can supply a lot of written materials to support this effort. Sales reps and distributors can even do some of the legwork in researching information to present to clients. Even if the topics are not interesting to you personally, you are helping these opinion leaders do their work better while they use you as a credible information source to quote or refer to. Your office will be known as the place to go for expert information. More important, this provides another natural conversation swing opportunity.

39. *Look for innovators among your clients.* Remember that these clients are most likely the opinion leaders. Ask them when they last tried a new product in your industry—and if so, which one. Ask them if they often try new products. You are looking for an opportunity to have them talk to their friends about a new product and about you. Ask a supply house to give you some marketing samples of a product you can use in word-of-mouth marketing, and give the product to your clients as a sample to test.

40. *Always focus on clients who have responded before.*   The most likely candidates for champion clients are those who have already referred others to you. A psychology professor once told me that the best predictor of future behavior is past behavior. If you have to rank your champion client list, put at the top those who have already referred clients. If you have limited resources to spend on word-of-mouth marketing, start by spending those funds on clients who have championed your business in the past. It is the champion clients who build your reputation.

41. *When you make changes based on suggestions, always tell your champion clients.*   This is another variation on keeping clients informed, and it shows that you take suggestions and complaints seriously. Simply placing a small typewritten notice at the reception desk, by the cash register or by the suggestion box will let clients know that you responded to their suggestions.

42. *Ask clients who they rely on or how often others rely on them for advice regarding products and services.*   Do others regard them as a good source of information on your products? How often do other people ask them for their opinion? The answers to these questions will help you identify the leaders.

43. *Don't ignore the socially isolated.*   Provide the same quality of service for everyone. If you make a point of serving those who are less socially active, you can leverage this community service to your advantage. Remember that these people are linked to others through casual acquaintances.

44. *Look for more opportunities to swing conversations to your advantage.*   Here are a couple of ideas: (1) Discuss a magazine article or videotape with a champion client; then give a copy to the client to give to someone else. (2) Send direct mail to champions informing them about new developments in your business—new systems, new procedures and new products that benefit them and their friends. Ask them to ask someone else's opinion of these improvements and report back to you.

45. *If you are a service professional, take your top referral agents out to dinner.*   You can host such a dinner in a restaurant or at your home, whichever is more comfortable. Allow plenty of time for informal talk at the dinner, making sure to visit with each person before, during or after the meal. Then make a formal presentation (you can use a prepared script) recognizing each guest separately for what he or she has added to the business. If you talk without a script, have someone from the office take notes on the specific things you say about each person. If you need help generating this presentation, ask your employees for their ideas.

This formal presentation is a natural time to tell clients that you value their support and that what they say about your business is important. Follow the meal with a personal thank-you note summarizing what you appreciate about each client. This is a powerful way to say thank you and is a lot less expensive than buying gifts. I attended a dinner where this type of appreciation was shown to a small group, and I could feel the appreciation that was generated.

46. *Give new product samples to a group of opinion leaders/champions, and ask them to discuss the product with their friends and family.*   Ask them to report back to you about the responses they get. You may be able to get these new products at no charge if you tell the manufacturer about the word-of-mouth marketing experiment you are conducting. Or you might use existing products (possibly donated by a manufacturer or supplier) that are available on the retail level. As a last resort, you can even describe new product ideas you or your staff read about in journals or heard about from associates. Ask the clients for a commitment to talk about the product with others and report back to you.

When they report back, ask with whom they spoke. This will give you an indication of the types of people these champions talk with. If they come to your business and have not reported back on their conversations regarding the product, remind them about their commitment and let them know you are interested in what they find. Why will this help you? What you are doing is creating a natural conversation swing toward a topic you want them to talk about with their friends: you and your business.

47. *Play the business trivia game.*   One month each year or one week each month, conduct a trivia quiz to determine which customers know the most about your business. This paper-and-pencil quiz can be implemented in the reception area. It serves two purposes: (1) It will tell you who has the most knowledge about the business (remember that those who know more about your business have more to say and will be listened to more often), and (2) it will give more information to clients who don't know very much about the business but would be eager to talk about you if they knew more. Pick interesting tidbits of inside information that add credibility to your business. Include such items as the following:

- The educational background of key personnel
- Special awards or recognition received
- How long the business has been serving the community
- The number of families with at least two generations in the business
- Community services
- Difficult problems you have been successful in solving for customers
- A few humorous bits of trivia as long as they are in good taste and cannot be used as negative word of mouth

People like trivia games and like to have this information when they talk to their friends. Reward clients who get high scores on the trivia games by

- personally commenting on how well they did.
- asking them how they learned so much about the business (you will find out more helpful word-of-mouth marketing information here).
- giving them a complimentary gift.
- sending them a personal note acknowledging their high scores and reinforcing the value of this knowledge for the business.

Making up trivia games can be fun for the entire staff. (This will help inform the employees, too, and add credibility in their eyes.) It does take time, but the payoff of well-informed clients and employees will be enormous. Make sure you get to see each version of your business trivia game before the clients do.

48. *Conduct more in-depth research on your clients' social networks when it seems appropriate.* A strong social network is also an indication that a client is an opinion leader or knows a few opinion leaders. To help you determine the strength of a client's social network, inquire about his or her family and close friends. Ask such questions as the following:

- Do you have regular, consistent contact with other people in your community? What types of groups or people?
- Among the people you know, who are some of the most capable, active individuals who are concerned with our products or services?
- Who would you pick (you may include yourself) to represent your circle of friends in a discussion about our products or services?
- Do you invite people over for parties or just to relax at your house?
- Are you involved with any clubs or organizations? Do you hold an office or lead in some way? What type of work do you do for that group?
- How much do you find other people coming to you for advice on shopping matters? Do you find that you have a lot to say about certain products? Which ones?

Take note of which family members and friends they are most likely to talk to. Take into account the client's age, social setting, proximity of residence, offspring, siblings, gender, etc. If your customer is not the family matriarch or patriarch, ask the client to bring this important person in so you can meet him or her personally. When this opinion leader comes in, celebrate by giving him or her the grand tour and introductions to your employees. Tell this person how much you appreciate having his or her offspring as a customer.

49. *Find ways to thank clients who support your positive reputation.* You can hardly go wrong with verbal and written statements of gratitude. When it comes to gift giving, however, be careful not to give a present that is too expensive. If your champion customers think the value of your gift is too high, they may suspect your motives. If you choose to use a gift-giving program to thank those who support your reputation, make the gifts modest. I'll say more about showing gratitude later.

50. *Give your opinion leaders more information within a week of their transaction with you.* This is the time they are most likely to think about talking with someone else. If you can reinforce this impulse with more specific information about their recent purchase, it will encourage them to talk. Try these ideas: a reminder of the benefits of their purchase, a word of gratitude for their patronage, a reminder of how the product or service can be used, further instructions on the product's use, or a reminder about after-sale services you offered.

51. *Give marketing mavens a chance to compare.* In your store or business, display information about the value and prices you offer compared with those of your competitors. Make simple charts, and highlight the main features and benefits with check marks or color. Print smaller versions of these charts to give to market mavens for themselves and for their friends.

52. *Give them extra information about the local market.* Nothing pleases a marketing maven more than to gather a great amount of marketplace information in a short time. You can be seen as a valuable source for these mavens if you do some of their research for them. Talk to your friends in the local business association or chamber of commerce to find some of the obscure "best deals around," then publish a small, one-sheet newsletter just for opinion leaders and marketing mavens. Change the information as often as you can (at least once a month, or more often if you have the time). Create a point-of-purchase display with the informative newsletters available. Encourage your shoppers to give them to friends or neighbors. Be sure to include one of your products as one of the "best deals around" in the newsletter.

53. *Take care of your influential patrons.* It pays to stay current on a wide variety of interests yourself so that, when influentials come into your business, you can interact with them at a level they find stimulating and helpful. Collect opinion papers from senators and members of Congress. Interview your local city council members and print summaries of their opinions. Conduct research in your industry and reserve this inside scoop for your influentials. Dole this information out at purchase events (or after they recommend someone to you) as a reward to influentials. If you put the proper spin on this data, you can enhance your company's position in the process.

54. *Become an opinion leader for your opinion leaders.* Opinion leaders have their own leaders to whom they look for advice. If you are consistently available to provide the information they seek (especially as it relates to products in which they are interested or to the marketplace, such as where to get the best deals), these opinion leaders will think of you when they are asked for information.

55. *Create a friendly atmosphere for product enthusiasts.* They like nothing better than to find a store that caters to their need to soak up information and new ideas. If you have a business that has even one section allocated to products of interest to enthusiasts, design the section for browsing and demonstrations. Fill it with current printed information on the products. Train at least one person on your staff to become an expert on the product. This individual must have an interest in people and in talking with other experts. Keep current merchandise available for enthusiasts to see in action.

56. *Start a mail-order profit center.* Product enthusiasts know a lot more about the products of their interest than the average consumer. They know the quality they want and the features that are required for quality. Many of these enthusiasts are as concerned about price as others. They are more willing to trust mail-order operations, because they know exactly what they are buying. Face it: Some of these enthusiasts are browsing in your store and buying through mail order. They enjoy reading catalogues. And many of these individuals participate in clubs or organized interest groups (you can find them). Start gathering names and addresses of people who browse or telephone with inquiries. Start small, with a one- or two-page product list, and expand as the interest grows.

57. *Help leaders identify product differences.* Opinion leaders believe that there are significant differences among competing products. Don't assume, however, that they will see those differences immediately. Tell them, write it for them, show them the differences.

58. *Form a product review panel.* This tactic has been used with some product categories to create opinion leaders for new products, but it also can be used for existing products. Here's how it works. Choose individuals with social leadership characteristics and ask them to be a part of a new product review panel. In consideration for their participation three or four times a year, the panel members get to keep samples of new products free of charge. Use written invitations and a telephone marketing campaign to recruit panel members. Emphasize that they can participate as often as they wish and that the participation is totally voluntary. In exchange for the free product they receive, they will be asked to try the product themselves. They will also be asked to show the product or discuss the new product with others. Finally, panel members will be given a short written survey for each product they receive. Panel members can also bring to panel meetings any other information they have. At each panel meeting, conduct a discussion of the product and hand out new products for the next review period. If they fail to attend the panel meeting, however, they owe you part of the cost of the product. When they attend the panel meeting, they sign a new agreement for the new product you deliver to them. Getting free products is a magnet for innovator-type people. You may have to establish a maximum number of panel members who can participate.

Chapter 4

*T*aking Advantage of Customer Clusters

"There is as much greatness of mind in acknowledging a good turn as in doing it."

— *Seneca*

*A*s marketing has matured over the last two decades, so has the ability with which companies can target narrowly defined groups in the general population. Direct marketing has shown us that it is possible to carefully select a market niche, identify the decision-making consumers in that niche, create a product or service to meet what is sometimes a subtle, unspoken need and then, through promotional tactics, signal these consumers directly.

This process of selecting small, definable groups and then concentrating marketing resources on them is called *market segmentation*. To be more efficient and effective, marketers have been trying for years to put consumers into groups that exhibit similar needs or characteristics. For example, children and parents with children have needs different from those of seniors, and single, upwardly mobile professionals have interests different from those of teen-age consumers. We group consumers by age, gender, geographic location, opinions, lifestyles, attitudes and several other categories.

These segmentation approaches, however, miss the point of word-of-mouth marketing, because people who talk for you can be found in all segments of society (see Figure 4.1). The fact that people have white-collar jobs, live in a certain ZIP code or are over age 55 may have little to do with whether they talk about your company to others: Some do and some don't.

47

This doesn't mean you should throw out all your ideas for dealing with the traditional clusters of consumers you serve. The needs presented by each of these groups do not go away just because you are organizing a consistent word-of-mouth marketing program. However, it means that for word-of-mouth marketing on a day-to-day basis, you must think differently about everyone connected with the company.

What Are the Primary Word-of-Mouth Clusters?

Logical word-of-mouth marketing groups include the following:

- Quiet customers
- New customers
- Established/loyal customers
- Opinion leader/champion customers
- People who are not customers but who are opinion leaders

Each group requires the same basic marketing tactics: (1) providing quality products and excellent service to build positive word of mouth; (2) quick and responsive complaint-handling procedures to stop negative word of mouth; and (3) encouragement to talk to others.

The Quiet Customers

In word-of-mouth marketing, you will get the most leverage from those who are opinion leaders—the ones who extend your reputation. But not all consumers appear to be reputation builders; indeed, many are your customers simply because they listen to others. Don't assume, however, that there is nothing to be done with this group in regard to word-of-mouth marketing. If one of these consumers comes to your company and has a horrible experience, he or she can easily begin producing volumes of negative word of mouth. These consumers can be silent but deadly if you cross them. Also, just because they seem to be the quiet type doesn't mean they are introverted. They may appear to be introverts to you, but outside they blossom into word-of-mouth champions. Here is your Action Agenda for quiet customers.

*A*ction *A*genda

59. *Keep them coming back by providing high-quality and excellent service.*

60. *Resolve complaints quickly to stifle negative word of mouth.*

61. *Look for more evidence that they are opinion leaders in disguise.* If they are opinion leaders in purchasing a kind of product or service different from yours, you may still have an opportunity to include them. Someone somewhere looks up to them for advice on what and where to buy things.

62. *Refuse to take them for granted.*

New Customers

New customers probably relied on the word of other people when deciding to come to your business. Now, however, they put these personal recommendations aside and begin judging for themselves whether their expectations match what you deliver. You feel good about having a new customer; you feel you have succeeded in your marketing efforts. You are looking forward to having a good proportion of these new customers turn out to be champions. However, they look at things differently. During the first purchase experience they are in a "wait and see" mode.

Even if they received a glowing report from a champion, their anxieties shoot up when they come to your company. The more difficult they perceive their own purchasing goals to be, the more anxiety they feel. If the problem-solving process is confusing, they feel anxious. If buying your product or service is a new experience, this adds to their anxiety. The anxiety also increases if it seems to take longer than expected to get a solution.

*A*ction *A*genda

63*. Have your staff acknowledge new customers enthusi-astically upon their arrival.*   A smile is not enough; a customer should be greeted with enthusiasm by the receptionist or clerk. It is easy for employees to screen customers' intentions before referring them to the appropriate personnel. From the consumer's point of view, this screening behavior is sometimes viewed as protecting the company. Instruct your staff to do the following things. First, find out the customer's name and then use it immediately and frequently in conversation. Take at least 60 seconds and get to know the person. Listen to his or her expressed desires. Be sure to thank consumers for entrusting their care to your office.

64*. Ask who they spoke with before deciding to purchase your product.*   It is not enough to ask, "How did you hear about the business?" You want to find out the names of current consumers who refer their friends to you. If a customer does not mention anyone, ask a couple of questions to find out who he or she is likely to talk to after visiting you. Ask yourself, "What does the age and gender of this person tell me about the kinds of people I am likely to encounter in his word-of-mouth networks?"

65*. Give plenty of reassurance if you see signs of anxi-ety.*   Talk to customers. Let them know that you and the office staff are there to help with any part of the experience, including questions they may have after they go home. Call your clients after the purchase to give additional instructions, answer their questions, offer additional information related or unrelated to their purchase, restate your guarantee or introduce them to someone in customer service.

66*. Begin looking for referrals.*   Do this discreetly at first, not aggressively. Timing can be crucial. If you try to create opinion leaders before they have a positive story to tell, you could very well turn them away. Why would you ask a new customer for a referral? Simply because people with problems to solve often speak with other people who have similar problems. Why not give the customer a chance to respond immediately by saying something like this: "Our business depends heavily on referrals from satisfied customers. Do you know anyone who should know about what we offer? Are you willing to send this person to me?" Some have been successful asking for specific names and phone numbers of these potential clients.

67. *Never pressure a customer for a referral.* Consumers will recommend you when they are ready. Goodwill is built upon trust. Until you have passed into the trust zone with your new clients, you have not built up goodwill. It is therefore more important to work at building trust than on pressing for a referral.

68. *Give the new customer the grand tour of the company, introducing all the key employees.* Introduce the customer by name each time (be sure to pronounce the name correctly). Celebrate the new customer. If you can find out early who referred the customer to you, emphasize this to all the staff members when you make the introduction, saying, "I'd like you to meet Martha Jones, a new customer who was referred by Mr. and Mrs. Brown." This way you are emphasizing several things at once: the new customer, the referring customer and the role the staff plays in creating happy consumers who send others to you.

69. *Give each new client a printed questionnaire.* New clients present an opportunity to gather information that will help you in your word-of-mouth marketing program. Some may not want to give you this information *before* you have developed their trust, so be prudent as to when you give it to new clients. Those in professional services will be able to gather helpful information on the first interview. This information can be detailed to include such things as other business professionals (if they relate to your work) who serve the client and information about his or her involvement in the community (remember that you are looking for leaders for your word-of-mouth marketing program). Retailers will need a much shorter questionnaire that will include name, address and referring customer. Create an incentive special offer, such as a gift drawing for which they register. If you intend to send them additional information about your store or its products, be sure to let them know.

70*. Give all new clients a printed resume.* Providing new customers with positive information about you before they receive your services will increase the chances of a positive experience. It helps reduce anxiety and builds positive expectations and trust in your competence. It also gives them something to share with others. Resumes can be available in waiting rooms of beauty salons, shoe repair businesses, new restaurants (offering information about the chef), dry cleaners, travel bureaus, or any business where clients have at least one minute to read something before they are served. If they have more knowledge about you, consumers will want to refer more friends and family members.

Ideally, the resume the customer receives should be on one small page (to fit in a purse, a pocket or a standard business envelope). Educational background, awards, professional affiliations, patriotic service and community activities are all appropriate information to include. Resumes of retail store managers, customer service managers or sales managers may be given with the receipt at the conclusion of the transaction. Resumes for retailers should emphasize their experience in dealing with people, along with evidence of their commitment to solving problems and maintaining positive customer relations.

71*. Create a special place in your business for new consumers to spend a few minutes before they meet you.* Here's how you can do it: Post thank-you notes from happy consumers on the wall, along with your resume on a larger-than-life poster. Put up another professionally made poster or sign that emphasizes your personal commitment to consumers and any guarantee you offer, your policy on solving problems and making things right, and an acknowledgment that most of your business is due to the reputation that other consumers have created for you in the past. Use a separate corner or section of the wall to display photos that indicate your involvement in the community.

72*. If there is a suggestion box in this area, explain its purpose and ask customers to complete one of the cards.* Emphasize that getting information like this helps you maintain high-quality service for them and their family members and friends.

73. *After the transaction, take an extra few seconds to tell new customers how much you appreciate the opportunity to serve them.*   Be sure to refer to the customer by name at least twice.

74. *Conduct all sensitive conversations in a private setting away from staff members and other consumers.*   This creates a perception that you will listen to them carefully.

75. *Make sure the final good-bye is given formally by someone in authority.*   If you have a "new customer gift" program, this is the time to present the gift. Ask consumers if they have any questions about your products and services or about their experience that day. Does all this take time? Yes. No one ever said that excellent service is quick and easy. It is hard work, and you can never lower your level of professionalism. Your first job with new consumers is to get them to want to return as often as necessary. Your second job is to so overwhelm them with excellent service that they cannot help but tell someone else about you.

76. *Record on tracking forms the marketing information about who consumers talked with when deciding to come to your company.*   Make notes in consumers' files on the significant people in their life and whom they are likely to talk with after the visit.

77. *Note the company where your customer's spouse works.* Here is another natural network of friends and associates. Spouses are as significant as the customer in the word-of-mouth process.

78. *Send follow-up letters to the person who referred the customer to your business.*   The "thank you for your referral" letter should be as carefully crafted as any marketing letter. Even if it is a hand-written note, it should be well thought out in advance. Sample thank-you letters can be kept on file to speed up the process.

79. *Send a "welcome to the company" letter.*   This can be personalized to each customer's situation even if you draw upon form letters you have used in the past.

80. *Do something completely astounding.*   If you gather telephone numbers, call a new customer on the telephone the next day. The call must be kept short, with a tidbit of information, a reminder about a key part of your services or your guarantee, information about new products or services, or simply a statement that you are glad they chose to come to your business.

81. *Develop a new-customer gift program.*   Here are some ideas: a copy of a magazine, coffee mugs, writing pens and other promotional items, magnetic note pads, information videos (on loan to marketing mavens), coupon for free or discounted service for a friend, sample products.

82. *Give new consumers helpful information on how to use your business.*   This can include information about the service department, special-order desks, mail-order programs and other services, and whom to call for what. Give them information on what to do when something goes wrong, the hours you are open for business and unusual knowledge that you may have. Avoid making photocopies of photocopies, however, because this usually results in poor quality.

83. *Give them information on other related businesses.*   You are doing them a great service by making recommendations for other companies you trust. Consumers are looking for this but may not ask you for it.

84. *Praise the person who sent the new client to you.*   Before the new customer leaves, say something positive about the person who recommended your business. Comment on how nice it is to do business with him or her, or how much fun it is to have that person drop in. Remember that people talk, and this small bit of praise will surely get back to the referring customer. This is a good time to reinforce the concept that "our most important asset is our reputation in the community, and it is a pleasure to know that Mr. and Mrs. Brown play an important part in spreading the company's reputation by referring others." In addition, new customers who hear this glowing report will get the idea that you will say something similar about them to others.

85. *Ask new customers for a letter of recommendation.* If you get into the habit of asking for these testimonial letters, you will build a file that you can draw upon later for other ideas. To ask for such a letter, say "We routinely send out letters of recommendation to prospective clients who are considering our services. We like to keep this file of letters current. Would you be willing to write a short letter to us specifying what you liked about our service?" When they send you the letter, be sure to send them a thank-you note summarizing how important this letter is to you and that you value their contribution to your reputation. Surprise them by including a discount coupon or other appropriate gift.

86. *Bargain for testimonial letters in exchange for products or services at a discount.* This is especially important when your business is new and unknown. Tell your new customers exactly why you need their letter: "I am building a portfolio of references and need your letter to encourage other customers. I'm willing to offer a small discount in exchange for your letter saying how satisfied you are with our services." Be sure to get their firm commitment. You may even want to sign a simple agreement with them. If they are tardy in fulfilling their obligation, don't hesitate to remind them.

Established, Loyal Customers

These consumers can be the question marks: Are they champion referral agents or not? The biggest temptation is to take them for granted. They have been making purchases from you for years, but you have no evidence that they actively talk about your company. In this group there are a few champions you have not identified yet. Your task is to identify them and begin giving them champion acknowledgments. It may take time; however, if you look carefully, you may find many champions.

*A*ction *A*genda

87. *Have a heart-to-heart talk with champions.*   Tell them that you know they have been customers for a long time. This simple recognition is a powerful symbolic goodwill gesture.

88. *Seek their complaints.*   You will hardly ever hear a word of complaint from loyal consumers. So solicit any complaints in a positive manner, and reward consumers when they tell you how your service could be improved.

89. *Ask for referrals.*   It's okay to ask for referrals. You may get some from unlikely sources. When a customer comes through with a referral, give him or her a champion customer reward.

90. *Ask their advice on how to improve your word-of-mouth campaign.*   Champion customers will think of people who should know about your products and will suggest community groups to network with.

91. *Survey customers' purchasing patterns and recommend additional services.*   All companies have a standard set of products and services that they recommend for each type of customer they serve. Look at the pattern of your clients' purchases and identify those who could be buying more from you. Audit your self-referral protocols and determine how to expand this service to enhance consumers' convenience. Most of them will appreciate it and be glad that you took the time to be thorough. The same applies for any new service you initiate. You or an employee can develop a short verbal suggestion that the customer should have the new service performed, stating the reasons. Consumers have the right to decline the offer, but even if they do, they will appreciate the fact that you told them.

92. *Find out if you are getting only one person from the family or social group.*   Ask the customer where the other significant group members buy products or services in your category. If the customer tells you they go to other companies, let him or her know that you would consider it a privilege to serve them as well.

93. *Network with companies through your consumers.* An audit of your files will tell you which companies your customers are employed by. You can simply ask your regular, loyal patrons if they know others at work who need your services (for example, people new on the job who have just moved in from out of town). Have one of your staff ask how you might attract more customers at the same company. Let consumers offer to tell others personally or put up notes on the company bulletin board telling about your services and their experiences. If they offer to do this, support their efforts with business cards, brochures and a special discount for the first purchase these new customers make. When they respond with referrals, reward them as you would reward all of your opinion leaders.

Confirmed Champion Customers

Champions can surface from the ranks of new consumers quickly. If new consumers meet the criteria for an opinion leader, don't wait for them to go through the normal stages of becoming an established customer before enlisting them to talk for you. Why wait? Study the opinion leader criteria again and keep on the lookout for these types of people. When one comes in, go into action.

Champion consumers can take time to develop for two reasons: (1) It takes time to identify them as opinion leaders, and (2) it takes time to develop the goodwill. Remember that they know a lot about your business simply because they have been around a long time. They have settled into a routine of purchasing your products. These long-term champions believe in you so much that they want you to succeed as if you were family. They not only talk about you to others, they also promote you and become your advocates when they hear negative word of mouth.

*A*ction *A*genda

94. *Keep champion consumers informed.* When you have to be late, one of your employees should tell these customers where you are and the reason for the delay, then offer something to compensate for the inconvenience. If you are very late, have the staff keep the customer informed and offer to reschedule the appointment. If the customer has an urgent need for services and you are not available, refer him or her to another business. Then follow up with that business to confirm the referral and give an explanation. It is best if you establish relationships with other companies in advance so that the cooperating business will act in a routine, positive manner when it receives the referral from you. If the wait is at the end of the day, consider giving a gift certificate for lunch or dinner to valuable champion consumers as a way to make up for the inconvenience. Your champions will enthusiastically support you if you respect their honor, time and money.

95. *Keep close to them.*   Pay attention to your consumers' needs, and let them know you appreciate their support of the business. Communication is the key for opinion leaders. If they get a couple of extra minutes with you to talk about whatever is on their minds, they will appreciate it. If they see that you are really listening to them, they will be pleased. They look up to you as an authority figure. It means a lot when you pay attention to them.

96. *Acknowledge their thank-you notes.*   On one wall of the business, post the thank-you notes you get from champion consumers. Or, you can transcribe the notes so that they are more easily read. Typing the notes gives you a chance to edit out any information that should be kept confidential. Call it the wall of champions or the wall of fame to draw attention to it. A subhead can explain that these notes are from valued consumers who thought highly enough of the company to refer their friends and families. In this case, you are not the champion or the famous one. You are drawing attention to the consumers by acknowledging their contributions to your business through word of mouth. The notes can be about you, your staff or the whole office.

Don't have any thank-you notes? Start asking for them from your champion customers. Why will a wall of fame work? It gives champion consumers great pride to see their thank-you notes acknowledged and valued. It gives them something else to talk about to their friends. It is a momentous testimony for new customers who are waiting for your services. If you don't want to post the notes on the wall for some reason, just put them in a three-ring binder titled *Our Customer Hall of*

Fame, and let it quietly sit where customers wait. The first page of the book should be a personal letter from you explaining how valuable these consumers are to the company.

***97**. Guarantee your service.*   Only recently has the professional service industry become serious about offering guarantees. If you guarantee that champion consumers will never have to wait more than 30 minutes to see you, and you back up that offer with your dollars, you will have enthusiastic consumers who will brag about the business to others. However, you must be prepared to back up your guarantee with money to make it right for the customer. There are a lot of things you can do, such as offering a product at half price, or offering tickets for two for lunch or the theater, a magazine subscription, or something else of value. Above all, don't keep the guarantee a secret in the hope that no one will cash in on it.

***98**. Find something extra to do.*   Here is another great idea to keep champion consumers talking about how much they appreciate your service. Have a cabinet in your office designated as the champion cabinet; it should contain a videotape lending library, a magazine article cache or a collection of sample products. You may wish to adjust the contents of the cabinet seasonally to reflect the changing needs of consumers. In the summer months you can have two or three starter kits for a family barbecue or back-to-school kits to give children in August, before they shop for school supplies.

***99**. Call your champion consumers when least expected to tell them they are highly valued.*   You can quickly divide a written list of champion consumers and call a few each week. The phone call can be about your products; it can be a reminder concerning your advice; or it can be an acknowledgment of something important in their lives (graduation, anniversary, birthday, wedding, birth, career accomplishment). It can also be a very short call to let them know that you appreciate their support of your reputation in the community.

***100**. When it is appropriate, write a thank-you letter to other significant people in the life of your champions.*   There is nothing as gratifying as knowing that someone wrote your supervisor or boss and proclaimed loudly what a pleasure it was doing business with you. Putting in a good word with your champion customer's immediate supervisor will create more goodwill and probably spark a conversation about your services—another conversation swing opportunity. Be aware, however, that many consumers want their purchase behaviors to be kept confidential.

101. *Ask confirmed champions for referrals.* These champions will gladly respond, because they know you appreciate them. Many businesses will grow if the proprietor will simply ask for referrals from consumers who are talkers. When you ask for referrals, you do not need to provide an incentive. For example, if a champion customer refers another opinion leader who then becomes established as a customer, you could surprise him or her with a gift certificate for dinner for two or theater tickets for two. Use Figure 4.1 to identify in your own mind the kinds of people your champion clients are most likely to talk to. For example, if your champion is a female product enthusiast with a growing family, who is she most likely to talk with? If you are not sure, ask someone to brainstorm with you for ideas.

102. *If you make a mistake, correct it immediately.* Don't say "I'll look into the matter and talk with the office manager tomorrow" unless you really cannot resolve the matter without that person. Loyal consumers are not out to rip you off. They may sometimes misunderstand a situation, or you may make an error. No problem. Just correct it quickly. The faster you give the solution, the more likely it is that they will be overwhelmed with gratitude and will talk about it with someone else.

103. *Provide just-in-time service.* This will bond consumers to you, and they will talk about it to their friends at work. Here's how it works. Every time you have a champion customer scheduled to come into the office, have his or her name marked with a star or another symbol to alert the receptionist. At just the right time before the appointment, have the receptionist call to give the customer an update of how close you are to being on schedule. If you are running 15 minutes late, let the customer know. If you are an hour late because of an emergency, call ahead of time so they can adjust their work or errands to meet the change. Customers will love you if they can get extra work done before coming to the office. Let them know that you will call on the appointment day to tell them how close to schedule you are. Find out what phone number to use (home, work, etc.). If they will not be accessible, encourage them to call you about 30 minutes in advance of the appointment to check.

104. ***Personalize your statements of gratitude and acknowledgments for referrals.*** Do this by focusing on your own feelings. For example, you can feel honored, inspired, elated, grateful, delighted, enthusiastic, confident, eager, expectant, contented and proud. Don't use a generic phrase, like "I feel good about having you as a customer." This is overused and communicates nothing. Be specific about your feelings and the customer will get the message loud and clear.

Other Opinion Leaders

Your goal is to leverage all your business relationships with prospective customers. There are a variety of people who have contact with you and a host of potential consumers. These people include your physician, your insurance broker, the real estate agency, a taxi driver, the pharmacist, school administrators, the family dentist, professional consultants and a host of others.

*A*ction *A*genda

105. ***Get to know these referral sources by name.*** Only by developing a personal relationship with this network will you be able to build the trust necessary to generate referrals.

106. ***Evaluate whether you want to be associated with them.*** Ask yourself: Would I want my consumers patronizing this business? How will making referrals to this company affect my reputation?

107. ***Ask for referrals and offer to make referrals to them if they are in business.*** You can also offer to do other favors in areas where you are an expert. For example, I always offer to provide a complimentary consultation on word of mouth to either the company that recommends someone to me or to another company of their choice. This gives them a chance to do a favor for someone else. It also extends the network to a new cluster.

108. *Immediately reward all referrals verbally and in writing.* The longer you wait, the more difficult it becomes to acknowledge the referral. Long waits create anxiety and communicate to your loyal supporters that they are less important to you than they thought and than you may have indicated.

109. *Look to your employees for access to several hundred people you don't even know yet.* If they like the quality of your work for consumers, they will become willing referral sources. They see what goes on behind the scenes when consumers are not around. If you display ethical behavior during the private times, they will refer their friends and families. Ask them about the organizations they belong to and how you can attract consumers from those groups, or if they can think of a way to spread the word about your business. If they hesitate, they may have seen something they don't like, or perhaps they don't understand the impact your word-of-mouth marketing efforts have on consumers.

110. *Cultivate other business neighbors as potential sources of referrals.* You can develop cross-promotional programs in which you display their business cards prominently if they agree to do the same. Be sure to check out these business owners carefully first, so that your level of trust and confidence will be high. When you refer someone to their business, let them know who it was and when the referral occurred. If the referral arrangement turns out to be a one-sided affair, with you giving all the referrals, you don't have to continue referring to them. Contact all the businesses in your office building, or those that are geographically close to you. Also contact other businesses your prospective clients are likely to patronize.

111*. Solicit referrals from professionals.* Get to know them first, and then offer to do cross-promotional efforts (passing out business cards, sharing the costs of coupons for discounted services, etc.). Introduce yourself to receptionists and office managers. Meet some of these people for lunch, and take along a few resumes and business cards. Creating and maintaining referrals from other professionals involves getting to know them personally and discussing issues that are important to them (accomplishments, personal battles won, personal interests, etc.). If you value their referrals, do the following on a consistent basis: Take them out to eat, be available, respond immediately when they have a professional favor to ask, keep in constant communication on consultations you perform for them, thank them for their referrals and check the results of your marketing program. Track the results by keeping a small note card in your pocket or a sheet of paper on your desk with the names of referring professionals and the number of referrals per month they send you. With this chart, you can check for changes in referral patterns. If you notice referrals dropping off, see them in person immediately to evaluate the situation. Are they simply slow that month, or were they on vacation? Remind them that you are available anytime they need help on a case. If you keep in close contact with them, you will know when they plan to go on vacation, and you can ask them who is covering for them. Then make contact with their associate to let him or her know you regularly take referrals from the vacationing professional and are glad to help while your friend is gone.

112*. Establish relationships with community service organizations.* These include foundations, social service agencies and government-sponsored agencies. The key people to know here are the managers and those who actually deal with clients. These people should have your resume and be given the grand tour of the office, meeting all the key employees. Make a commitment to promote their organizations among your consumers. Offer to give speeches or in-service educational talks to their staffs. Offer to be on the advisory board of one or more of these groups. Make a donation to the cause.

If you do any of these things, they will love you and become champions for you. Here is a starter list of the types of organizations to consider:

- The local executives club
- Rotary Club, Lions Club, etc.
- The downtown business association
- A chamber of commerce program or networking club
- City social services facilities advisory board

If you participate in any of these organizations, make sure you are consistent and dependable. Get involved with their agendas and make it a point to develop relationships in which you can help others network. If you do favors for these other businesspeople, you will be storing up for yourself a huge bank of goodwill that you can call upon for new business. If, however, you join one of these groups and talk of nothing but your business or are constantly asking for referrals right from the start, you will face an uphill road to goodwill.

Building Opportunities Using the Word-of-Mouth Matrix

After making a list of where referrals come from for your business, complete the following four steps using the matrix in Figure 4.1.

1. Assign a matrix category to each referral source.
2. Place a check mark (or write an estimate of the percent of referrals generated) on the matrix for each category of opinion leaders with which you are currently most effective.
3. Identify on the matrix the other categories of people through whom you desire to spread your reputation. Think about the types of people these potential referral sources are most likely to talk to.
4. As you read this book, make a list of the activities that will improve your word-of-mouth marketing with either current or new referral sources.

FIGURE 4.1 Word-of-Mouth Matrix

Customers	Opinion Leader	Market Maven	Influential	Product Enthusiast
Quiet customers (?)				
New customers (gifts)				
Loyal customers (pillars)				
Confirmed champions (stars)				
Offended customers (time bombs)				

Others

	Opinion Leader	Market Maven	Influential	Product Enthusiast
Casual acquaintances				
Business friends				
Close friends				
Industry leaders				
Industry players				
Ethnic group members				
Age				
Gender				
Race				
Education				
ZIP Code				
Occupation				
Income				
Lifestyle				

$\mathcal{S}$topping Negative Word of Mouth

*"*No one is perceived as being more honest than when they criticize you.*"*

— *Bernard Taylor*

*"*There is nothing that can't be made worse in the telling.*"*

— *Terence*

$\mathcal{L}$earning from negative word of mouth can be one of the most positive parts of your word-of-mouth marketing program. For example, some of your most loyal customers are those who bring you legitimate complaints that you solve quickly. If you do more than listen and apologize, if you really bring a solution, you create a bond with them that can last through the years. And you give them a reason to talk with enthusiasm about how great you are.

Forming an opinion about a new business happens the moment a prospective customer is exposed to the smallest bit of information about your company. Their first impressions are formed through exposure to your location, your company sign outside the building, your letterhead, how you and your employees dress, the appearances of other customers, smells, sounds and many other types of stimuli. But until they have reason to think otherwise, prospective customers are prone to have positive attitudes about something that is new.

Complainers: Allies or Pests?

Consumers are improving their ability to shop and get good deals. Senior citizens are seasoned shoppers with years of experience; they know when someone is giving them the runaround. Younger, more educated consumers are more likely to voice their displeasure with problems.

In the final analysis, customers are your economic bread and butter. Your business exists because of them. The majority are kindhearted and good-natured, and would not wish you harm under normal circumstances. In fact, most are willing to help you with information that will help you serve them better. They are your best allies as well as your best marketing resource. If you catch yourself thinking of a customer as a pest, ask yourself these three questions:

1. Why is this customer so upset? Is there something else going on here that I don't understand? Have I said or done something that made matters worse?
2. If this customer leaves the company in an angry state, what negative word of mouth will result? Does this person have an extensive social network? Is this customer a natural opinion leader to whom others look for advice?
3. Why don't I see this customer as an ally to help us improve the quality of service?

Rumor Mills and Why They Exist

Rumors get started when

- a dissatisfied customer experiences an unresolved problem.
- your paid promotional messages distort reality.
- competitors attempt to discredit you.

Some people spread rumors to relieve the tension they feel as they process the information. Others pass along information in the hope that they will bring closure to a confused situation. Their natural curiosity for a rational explanation drives them to explore the situation with others. Still others, through participation in rumors, find in other people's behaviors an explanation for their own feelings. This projection on others is no help to you, but it is a way for some people to protect themselves from facing their own feelings. For another group of rumor spreaders, talk is a way to get attention, fill conversations with entertainment value, or maintain a perception of prestige by sharing information that others do not have.

Some rumors will die of their own weight. Over time, most who hear the rumor either are uninterested or their interest is short-lived. Other rumors are destructive and should be dealt with openly. In this case, the worst thing that can be done is to act as if it didn't exist. The next worst thing is to belittle the importance negative word of mouth has for your company.

Implement a Complaint-Gathering Program

In one company where I helped put together a customer service program, the employees were told that they should reduce the number of complaints from customers. Because that sounded like one of the best things a company could do to improve its internal marketing, the supervisors set about educating the employees regarding top management's goals.

I watched with interest as the program started. Employees found ways to minimize the chances that customers would lodge formal complaints. They patronized the unsuspecting, made it difficult for people to get in a word, apologized and made promises to the most vocal customers that things would improve or were not as they seemed. Worst of all, they stopped asking for feedback from customers. Some even refused to report complaints—all in an effort to fulfill their supervisor's request. The result: Top management achieved its goal. The number of complaints sent to top management decreased.

Unfortunately, the number of dissatisfied customers *increased.* Customer relations became a game of eluding the inevitable. This created a high-tension work situation in which employees did whatever it took to minimize the chances of complaints.

Only when top management changed its goal were complaints viewed as the positive resource they really are.

Complaints are the best way to educate and motivate employees about what needs to be done to make things better. They are the only way specific changes can be made to prevent making more dissatisfied customers. I recommend actively looking for problems to correct, for the following reasons:

1. If you don't know the specific problems customers experience, how will you be able to fix them?

2. If you are not talking to your customers in a way that allows them to be open with you, how will you be able to meet their changing needs?

3. Customers who have a chance to talk with you about a problem are much more likely to remain loyal.

4. Generating complaints and responding to them creates a corporate culture that is focused on the customer.

Your complaint-gathering program is your way of taking the pulse of the customer community. Without such monitoring, you can lose touch with reality very quickly. Remember that only a minuscule portion of your customers will tell you when they are upset, irritated, disappointed, frustrated or angry.

Complaint-gathering programs come in a variety of forms. It doesn't matter which approach you select as long as you are consistent and the method you choose fits naturally with your approach to business. Here are some of the typical methods companies use to gather complaints.

*A*ction *A*genda

---

113. *Use the telephone to call customers the day or evening after their purchase.* Ask them if they found the service satisfactory. Was there anything you should know about the visit that will improve future visits? Were they treated courteously by all staff members? Were they able to get an appointment when they wanted it? Did you spend enough time with them? Did they think you and the staff were competent? Did anything leave them uncomfortable or uneasy?

114. *Use direct mail to survey customers one or two days after a visit.* Before customers leave the company, tell them they will receive a short survey in the mail. Ask for a commitment to complete it and send it back. Make sure the survey form is easy to complete. Also, include a postage-paid envelope for returning the form. A variation on this is to distribute the survey forms and postage-paid envelopes when customers leave the office, and ask for their commitment to complete the survey form and mail it back within 24 hours.

115. *Place suggestion boxes in strategic locations to gather helpful information.* If you use the suggestion box, do not make it a passive system. You can have a small poster by the suggestion box explaining why it is there, but you should personally inform all your customers what the suggestion box is for and ask for a commitment to complete the short card before they leave.

116. *Conduct a customer exit interview.* Use a few pre-pared questions similar to those suggested above for telephone interviews. Explain why you do exit interviews, and state that you value their suggestions for improving your service.

117. *Immediately interview a customer who seems upset.* If you notice nonverbal indicators that a customer is irritated, anxious, frustrated, angry or disappointed, take the customer into a private area for a discussion. Nonverbal flags to watch for include facial expressions, tone of voice and aggressive actions. Use opening questions to solicit feedback, such as the following:

- "I was noticing you here today, and I'm wondering if there is anything I need to know that will help us serve you better."
- "I want to make sure we do all we can to make your experience with us a positive one. Is there something I can do to make your visit better today?"
- "You seemed upset a few minutes ago. Is there something I can do to help make your visit more pleasant?"

Avoid asking "Is everything okay?" because most people will simply say yes and drop the matter quickly. That approach gets you nowhere if you are certain that the person is in fact upset about something. After you have stated that you are interested in a problem, if the customer still refuses to tell you what is wrong, don't push him or her into a corner. Just say, "If you ever think of anything that will make your visit here more pleasant, I will be happy to talk with you."

Customers must know what types of information you are gathering and why the information is important to you. You can openly link the surveys with the fact that you know they can refer other people to your company. They also have a choice in returning to you rather than going elsewhere. You value their patronage and want the relationship to continue.

118. *Log all complaints.* Use a notebook or file system to capture specific details of complaints and how they are resolved. Note in the log who handled the complaint, the date and time the complaint was received, and the date and time it was resolved.

119. *Categorize complaints into natural groupings.* Doing this will help you understand where the most glaring problems are.

120. *Inform your employees.* Let them read the log. At the monthly staff meeting, set aside time to identify new problems, solutions to unresolved problems and the results of solved problems.

121. *Post suggestion cards for customers and employees to see.* This is particularly effective when you post your response to suggestions right on each card. It reinforces the importance of the suggestion system and encourages everyone to participate.

Establish an "Instant Solution" Program

The faster you can respond to a customer's problem, the more likely it is that the customer will not even remember that there *was* a problem. The slower you are in responding, the more likely it is that the problem will become significant.

Think about it from a customer's point of view. If you received awful service and have cranked up the courage to confront someone about the problem, the last thing you want is to be told to wait for someone else to handle it. To an upset customer, waiting is like punishment for raising the complaint in the first place. The key is *speed*.

Most organizations are geared for a slow, methodical approach to solving consumers' problems. Formal procedures must be followed, including approval by specific people, time to research the options, time to confirm the details of the problem, time to analyze which part of the complaint is fact and which part fiction, an office discussion about the customer and the customer's "true" motives, and a careful rechecking of office policies to make sure you are not giving away the store.

I'm not suggesting that rules and formal policies be thrown out; I'm merely saying that a customer's complaints should be addressed quickly.

If you act instantly to solve the problem, you gain respect from the customer, avert a potential word-of-mouth disaster and walk away from the situation knowing you did your best. The longer you wait, the more you risk having the problem become more important to the customer than the original transaction.

Follow the advice in the next few Action Agenda items when developing your instant-solution program.

*A*ction *A*genda

122. *When a customer brings a complaint, quickly move to a private area to talk.*   This will help the customer relax and will communicate that you are interested in what he or she has to say. Answering the telephone in the middle of hearing a complaint will raise the customer's level of discontent. Employees walking in with questions unrelated to the problem will make the customer even angrier. Customers want to be heard. If you give them that, they immediately begin to relax, even if it doesn't show at first. Do not tell a customer "My employee will take care of it for you." Deal with the problem yourself.

123. *Explain in your own words what you understand the problem to be.*   You may be surprised that what you think is the problem is really not. Letting customers hear what you think gives them a chance to immediately correct errors in your understanding.

124. *Affirm your commitment to a satisfactory resolution.*   If you say this sincerely and then immediately act on it, the customer will calm down even more. He or she may even begin to trust you.

125. *Insist that the person who receives a complaint be the one to resolve it.*   Only under unusual circumstances should someone have to pass a problem on. When the employee has to check with upper management before resolving the matter, speed is of the essence. If you are in the middle of serving another customer, the customer with a complaint may have to wait a few minutes. In this case, the staff should explain the specific reason for the delay and find out whether it is acceptable to the customer to wait.

126*. Surprise the customer by acknowledging any mistakes you have made.*   Owning up to mistakes builds more trust. Most consumers are used to getting a runaround. Say "I'm sorry you experienced this problem, and I take full responsibility. I appreciate your bringing this to my attention so we can do something about it quickly." If you try to duck the problem by suggesting that someone else in the office probably made the mistake, the customer will feel that you are not interested.

127*. Tell the customer that you have the authority to make up for the problem right now.*   Offer a discount on the product or service or give the customer something to take home and enjoy. Before you make a specific offer, ask what he or she would like to see happen to rectify the situation. "What can I do to make it right for you right now?" (Note the continued emphasis here on an instant solution.) The customer may merely want to vent anger and leave with the sense that he or she was heard. Or the customer may want some financial consideration.

128*. If the customer wants nothing tangible, offer it anyway.*   If the customer says that he or she only wanted to let you know about the problem and needs nothing further, thank the customer sincerely. Then offer something of tangible value that confirms the importance of the complaint. You may think this is not necessary, but why not send the customer out of the office satisfied, happy *and* surprised? You will create positive word of mouth about your responsiveness.

129*. If the customer asks for something reasonable, honor the request immediately.*   This requires that you do some planning to establish the limits of what you are willing to give in consideration. If such customers are not sure what they want, make them an offer: "Would taking half off your expenses today be a fair way to settle it for you?" A promise of excellent service in the future is not, however, the solution to today's problem. The longer you wait to deal with the issue, the more the customer will want in consideration. The more quickly you can settle on something fair, the less you will spend in the long run.

_130_. _Reinforce the importance of the customer bringing the problem to your attention._   This is a great opportunity to tell customers that you value their trust and appreciate their patronage.

Implementing an instant-solution program will cost money occasionally. But think of the damage one person can do by spreading negative word of mouth about how unresponsive you are and saying that you don't care about your customers. Besides, you can set limits on what the employees can offer as an instant solution so they do not offer every complainer the moon.

Heading Off Problems Before They Begin

Prevention is the best cure for word-of-mouth problems, but it is human nature to wait until a problem arises before doing something about it. If something is not a known problem to customers, why change it and risk creating a problem you didn't count on? The answer to this question is three-pronged.

First, it may not seem like a problem yet simply because customers have not said anything about it. But they could be experiencing irritation, frustration or confusion. What do you think would happen if you removed these thorny irritations? Would they complain if you made their lives easier? I doubt it. They would probably say something about it the next time a conversation swing took them in that direction. Fixing a problem may be just the thing to start them talking positively about you to others.

Second, perhaps customers think that the problem is simply the way things are supposed to be in your industry. Their expectations have been so conditioned that it has never dawned on them that things could be different. Should you count your blessings? Not necessarily. This is a great opportunity to show how you are different.

Finally, if you wait until a problem shows up before you do something about it, it will be twice as hard to fix, because you will also have to take care of the negative feelings of the customer. This doesn't seem very efficient to me: It is a waste of valuable time and money.

*A*ction *A*genda

131. *Follow up on referrals to other companies.* Confirming that what was expected was actually received not only creates an opportunity to prevent misunderstandings, it also clearly communicates that you want things to go smoothly. If you expect as much of referral organizations as you do of your own company in regard to customer service, you will have happier customers, because they will have fewer encounters with other people's mistakes. Does it cost you? Yes. Is it worth it? Yes. I know some people think it's not their job to improve the customer service of the organizations to which they send customers, but if you don't help, it could eventually reflect negatively on you if something goes wrong.

132. *Train everyone in your business who might be in a position to receive a customer complaint.* I've intentionally called business offices at lunchtime or near closing time to see how the call is handled. You'd be surprised at what I hear. I'm routinely told by one company, "Can you call back in the afternoon when the manager is supposed to be here?" Another person will simply say, "I don't know. You'll have to call back later." She does not even offer to take a message. No wonder customers get angry. Proper training is the only way to prevent this type of word-of-mouth problem.

133. *Create a foolproof method to transfer information among the various people involved with the customer.* A small mistake in information transfer can cause great inconvenience for a customer. You need to create a system of checks and balances to minimize the risk of losing important information. Where are breakdowns in the system most likely to occur? Where are the weak links in the information chain? What can you do to correct these problems before you are faced with a public relations nightmare? What you are attempting to do here is to plug up those cracks through which things tend to slip at the most crucial time.

134. *Make changes visible and communicate them to customers.* This is similar to posting your responses to suggestion cards on the bulletin board. As you implement a problem-seeking program, you are bound to find at least a few things you can do differently to improve customer satisfaction. You may want to put a poster in an area where customers wait to be served.

135. *Telephone all known ex-customers.* Your purpose in calling them is to find out why they stopped buying from you. Listen to their suggestions. Make the changes you can to attract them back. *Ask* them to come back. Those who do come back should receive a special premium for their willingness to tell you how your operation can be improved.

136. *Model the idea that complaints are like gold.* If employees believe you are not interested in handling complaints yourself, they will not be motivated to handle them either. If they see you avoiding the task of looking for complaints, they will avoid it, too. If, on the other hand, you actively and visibly search for complaints in their presence, report on complaints you find and report on the outcomes of resolving those complaints, you give the clear message that complaint handling is the only way to change the company into a positive word-of-mouth marketing machine.

137. *Train your staff to show a willingness to listen.* Practice asking open-ended questions that make it easy for customers to comment specifically on your service. Instead of asking (like so many waiters and waitresses do) "Is everything all right?" say something like, "We are always looking for ways to improve our service here, and I am wondering what we need to know about your food or our service that can be improved." Or, "Tell me about one area where we can improve our service to you." These are open-ended questions that create an atmosphere of openness. They suggest that you value feedback.

138. *Start a service journal.* Ask your employees to write down things they see, hear or feel that are either real or expected customer complaints. This journal will, over several months, contain a picture of how your company is perceived. It is an anecdotal record of your position in the market. Make the journal easily accessible to employees (one copy for each work unit is the minimum). Anonymous journaling is a way employees can communicate with you on sensitive issues they may be afraid to confront directly.

139. *Have a heart-to-heart talk with your employees about customer feedback.*   Help them see that customer complaints are not ways to find and get rid of the "bad apples" in the business, but are simply feedback that assists the company in learning how to keep focused on customers. Feedback presents opportunities to change— and while change is sometimes uncomfortable, it often makes life easier for customers.

140. *Recognize that the larger your company is, the more complex your customer service system will be.*   This is a reality that many larger companies have refused to accept. Maintaining a customer focus is often defined as a once-a-year training program during which trainers tell employees what they should be doing. While this in itself is not bad, by itself it gives a message that nothing more is expected than showing up at the annual training program. If your company is large, your customer service program will be large and complex, taking into account the dynamics present within each diverse working unit and division. When training, recognition and feedback are part of a continual process at the working-unit level, then the company as a whole maintains its focus on the customer.

141. *When faced with a complaint, always ask, "What can we do to send this customer away happy?"*   In many situations, it is not enough to have a point person as the buffer for angry customers. Dissatisfied customers are not letting off steam for their health; they want tangible results. Similarly, it is not enough to have a standardized gift program that is implemented whenever a complaint is heard. This quickly degenerates into giving the gift just to get the customer out of your hair. I've seen this in restaurants, where complaining patrons were given dessert at no charge (not a bad idea in itself). The problem was in the attitude with which the waiter delivered the dessert. He made it clear he was not happy having to make the delivery. The patrons went away a little amused at the immature waiter, but also feeling like they were not taken seriously.

142. *Make customer service policies fair.* Make your complaint-handling policies consistent and fair. If customers see inequities, they suspect that they are not getting a fair response themselves.

143. *Match the solution to the level of risk to the consumer.* Riskier situations deserve proportionately more consideration.

144. *Make the process fair.* If the customer wants the problem reported up the line of command, don't assume that a simple gift will take care of it. The solution cannot be fair until the process becomes fair. Process fairness involves the exchange of information about the customer (strive to represent them fairly in all conversations) and about the problem; how the customer service employee uses the information; and whether the complaining customer feels like he or she has any influence over the outcome.

145. *Avoid punishing the customer.* Punishment comes in many forms: speaking rudely, nonverbal behaviors that reflect the customer service staff person's frustrations, using the tone of voice that says "I don't have time for this," etc.

146. *Present tangible solutions.* If the customer wants to have a problem passed up the line, do more than promise that it will be done. Bring in a supervisor and express the concern in his or her presence. If the customer simply wants an apology, give it immediately, then give the customer something else as a tangible reminder that you appreciate him or her bringing the complaint to your attention in the first place.

147. *Check with your lawyer and your liability insurance broker for ways to minimize your risks.* Nothing in this book is meant to take the place of the sound legal advice and good risk-management tactics that these professionals can provide.

148. *Follow these rules of thumb.*

- As the severity of the problem for a consumer increases, so does his or her tendency to engage in negative word of mouth.

- Opinion seekers assign more weight to negative product or service evaluations than they do to positive evaluations.
- Negative feelings customers have about your product or service occur in a moment, but they will last for years if you do not address them immediately.
- Most customers do not want to confront your company about things that make them dissatisfied, as they believe they will get no action or feedback. In addition, to complain requires them to face their own feelings.

149. *Sell durable, reliable products.* The longer a consumer owns a product, the less likely it is that he will engage in negative word of mouth if dissatisfaction occurs.

150. *Be genuine.* Consumers judge the degree of genuineness with which customer service representatives handle consumer complaints. The more genuine the response, the more positive a dissatisfied consumer will become.

151. *Be responsive.* Responsiveness is shown by providing easy access to people who can solve the problem quickly and efficiently. It is also shown by what consumers perceive as tangible resolutions to their complaints.

152. *Be personal.* The most persuasive messages along the word-of-mouth networks are the ones about personal experiences. If you give customers positive personal experiences, you are giving them reason to engage in the most powerful form of marketing. Impersonal customer service irritates customers.

153. *Be careful.* Every transaction places your customers in a vulnerable position that causes them to feel anxiety and awkwardness. Respect their position at all costs.

154. *Continue educating opinion leaders.* They are your best weapons to stop rumors that are not true. If you are not sure what they pass on to others, survey them to find out. If you hear that there may be a negative rumor (with false information) going around, find out the contents of the rumor, then give opinion leaders detailed information with which to combat it.

155. *Keep things simple when confronting a rumor.* When you explain things to opinion leaders or the public, use common terms instead of vague euphemisms. Explain your options. Give clear directions regarding what consumers can do about it.

156. *Develop a public relations crisis plan.* Much expense and personal grief can be avoided by having a crisis plan in place to guide you. If consumers are harmed because of negligence or tainted products, a crisis plan will be as much help from a marketing perspective as your lawyer is from a legal point of view. Most companies wait until the crisis hits them before they create a crisis plan.

Chapter 6

*B*reaking Through Cultural Barriers

*"*People talk.*"*

— American proverb

*"*Talk proceeds along bloodlines.*"*

— Anonymous

*7*he most significant cross-cultural challenge you face as a business owner involves your assumptions about clients from other cultures. Whenever a client comes in speaking a different language, dressed in unusual clothing and holding a different set of beliefs about life, you will be faced with this challenge.

These and other cultural traits make us what we are regardless of our heritage or the color of our skin. Frequently, the cultural traits of clients conflict with what you believe to be the accepted norm. When this happens, extra care is needed to prevent negative word of mouth and promote positive reports about your products.

Word-of-mouth reports are stronger than advertising within ethnic groups. In many cases, paid advertising totally falls flat because of the negative word of mouth: Too many stories have been told that create distrust and hesitation. What should be a response-getting communication piece results in no response from certain cultural groups because of negative word of mouth or because the advertising is out of touch with cultural dynamics among those maintaining their ethnic identity. Can you overcome this with more advertising? No. Can you solve it with culturally sensitive advertising? Maybe, but this isn't the total answer, because word of mouth is the primary source of credible information within ethnic groups.

Culture's Power

In North America, two forces are at work molding culture. The dominant culture, which already is a melting pot, encourages minority groups to blend into the American way of life. Because many people in ethnic and cultural subgroups want to share the American culture, they willingly accept this influence. As they borrow from American culture, their lives change and they become integrated with what they see around them.

The other force is the drive to maintain cultural identity. Ethnic heritage is powerful enough to maintain dietary and personal hygiene habits, core beliefs and family activities. When a client comes to your business, you don't know immediately whether that client is open to cultural assimilation or wants to maintain his or her cultural identity. It is a risk to assume the former.

Culture Is Learned Behavior

Culture has power in our lives, because we learn cultural and ethnic ways of behaving from infancy. We learn

- that some foods are acceptable and some are not.
- that certain symbolic and some practical tools and materials are needed in the household to carry on the normal routines of life.
- that some products and brands are more highly valued than others because of what they represent to the community.
- the language of the family.
- beliefs about how things should be.

Culture is taught to us explicitly by our significant family members and social leaders. It is taught implicitly by modeling behavior in our presence so that there will be no mistakes. Culture is also powerful because it is an integrated way of living and thinking. Ethnic identity is not merely a collection of things to eat, wear, do and say. It involves the internalizing of these things as well as what they mean to us.

People from all cultures also learn culturally accepted purchasing behaviors. They learn to give explanations for their purchases that are consistent with the whole community. Your clients may have a well-developed list of labels that describe their needs, but do not assume that they mean the same as they do in your culture.

Common Values Build Your Reputation

Fortunately, some common values cross cultural lines and span generation gaps. In general, people from all cultures value hospitality, though its practice may be slightly different in each culture. All cultures value giving and generosity, defined in their own terms. All cultures value obedience, learning, peacemaking and reciprocity. Use these common threads as links with your clients from ethnic groups other than your own. In other words, if you are not sure what to do in a situation, be sure to include healthy doses of hospitality, reciprocity, generosity and giving. If you do this, your positive reputation will precede you.

What To Watch For

If your business is in a metropolitan area, you know that pockets of ethnic subgroups are clustered in neighborhoods. Drive the main business streets and you can see the cultural influences of shop owners reaching out to their constituents. If you are not sure what the ethnic mix of your city is, contact the local library and ask to see the most recent reports from the U.S. Bureau of the Census. These reports will identify specific neighborhoods that have the highest concentrations of various cultural groups.

The close family ties among ethnic clients create a natural grapevine for your reputation. After a client visits your business, the whole family may get together to discuss the event. Besides their own interest in your product, you and your work are central to the discussion; this is word-of-mouth marketing at its best.

In every cultural group and for every product category, a dominant decision maker emerges as the primary target of marketing promotion efforts. Women, in many cultures, are the dominant force in purchasing food products, healthcare and clothing, while men may lead in purchasing other products. Start gathering information on your culturally identifiable customers. Who is the decision maker for your products? You may have some intuition about who this is from your experience with customers. Check with business owners in other neighborhoods to confirm your assumptions. Most important, check with your customers.

Identifying the Opinion Leaders

The constant challenge in word-of-mouth marketing is identifying the opinion leaders. This is especially true when you are attempting to build a reputation within an ethnic subculture. Here are some suggestions to help you in this process.

There are two types of cultural opinion leaders to on which to focus. Some people are the cultural innovators—the ones who are making an effort to assimilate into the dominant culture. These people maintain a close connection with their social roots but also go outside their own groups. They tend to be better educated and to have had more exposure to American culture. The greater the distance between themselves and their relatives who have immigrated, the more they will assimilate. They travel out of their neighborhoods and listen to American communications.

Most of these individuals are found in metropolitan areas, where they can experience the full range of American culture. They take classes in local colleges to improve their ability to interact with Americans. These cultural risk takers are followers of American culture. The people they have contact with in the mainstream culture are their opinion leaders. For many people, these opinion leaders represent what it means to be successful.

Those who follow the lead of cultural innovators also want to assimilate into the larger culture. They aspire to become successful and intentionally imitate the innovators. They accomplish this through repeated personal communication with innovators, by observing their behavior and by reading about the experiences of innovators and the results they achieve. This information encourages them to continue the quest and cautions them to avoid the problems others have encountered.

The other opinion leaders are the cultural traditionalists who are looking to maintain their cultural forms. They wish the innovators would use specific products and brands that incorporate the values of the community. Traditionalists may view innovators as prime examples of what to avoid. These individuals prefer their own language and sometimes refuse to speak English even if they are able. They are less likely to experiment with external cultural traits, such as food, clothing and entertainment. They may prefer to stay at home rather than go into what is perceived as a hostile environment. They highly regard cultural self-sufficiency and have strict codes of discipline.

*A*ction *A*genda

157. *Hire employees who are bilingual.* This is especially important in metropolitan areas where dozens of cultural subgroups live. Employees who speak the appropriate language can soothe clients' fears and anxiety. They can also be an ally in building confidence in your skill. Avoid using children to translate. When you do use a family translator, ask the person to translate word for word without interpretation. Also ask that person to seek clarification if there is any doubt about anything you say.

158. *Identify the cultural marketing mavens.* Marketing mavens live and work in every social group. Nowhere is this more true than within ethnic communities. Because these communities are so close, the marketing mavens have a tremendous power of referral. Follow the ideas I suggested in Chapter 3.

159. *Actively cultivate a relationship with local community leaders.* They can be some of your best referral sources if you have their trust. They also can block referrals and counteract your work if they distrust you. The best way to identify them is to get to know some of the families in the area. As trust develops between you and these families, they will feel more free to discuss their purchasing habits with you. Once you have identified the community leaders, make it a point to get to know them personally. If you are friendly and do not rush the relationship, they will like you, and this will begin translating into referrals. In turn, you can do them a favor by giving them up-to-date information about your industry and your products.

160. *When you develop a list of 10 to 15 community leaders, invite them to a free educational seminar.*   You are the featured speaker at this event, where you give them practical information on how to use your products and how to identify quality in your industry. Teach them practical things they can pass on to the community that depends on them for information.

161. *Give leaders complimentary products to develop referral bonds.*   Show them extra attention when they come into the business. Your generosity must be genuine, or you will be perceived as simply trying to use their relationships with others.

162. *If older members of the cultural group receive extra respect, give the same to your older clients.*   Practice politeness and warmth.

163. *Incorporate ethnic alternatives into your product recommendations.*   If you are unsure what you can suggest that is culturally acceptable, start talking to your customers. Listen to what they say about how your products are used and why they buy your products—what goals they are accomplishing and what problems they are trying to solve.

164. *Make sure to spend time with ethnic clients.*   They look up to business owners. Some will worry that because they are from a different culture, they will not get the same value for their dollar as American customers. Make sure you spend time listening to them during the transactions. Show your personable and warm side.

165. *Check your assumptions about the cultural groups represented among your clients.*   You are at risk if you make generalizations about all people in an ethnic group based on the behavior of just a few. Never assume that members of a cultural group are uninformed about your products. While they may not have been educated in an American school, they have learned to depend on marketing mavens and opinion leaders for product information and may know more about your products than do people in the dominant culture.

166. *Remember that individual differences exist among people within a cultural subgroup.* If the other suggestions aren't enough to keep you alert, this one will.

167. *Be sensitive to ethnic clients who may perceive greater risk in trying a new company for the first time.* If you give them a little extra time during the first few buying experiences, you will minimize their anxiety and build your credibility. Instruct your employees on this point. Help them remember that if you rush the service, you will leave these clients confused, disappointed and fearful, setting yourself up for negative word of mouth.

168. *Display your diplomas and certifications prominently.* Some people from other cultures see more value in the tangible evidence of your credentials. If you have published articles in the newspaper, make a bulletin board display of the first page of each article. If you give lectures at a school, college or community group, put up copies of announcements or programs that list the topics of your speeches. These can be silent reminders that you have the credentials to serve their needs.

169. *Be aware of the pride people have in their heritage.* Attend parades and festivals to discover important cultural traits. If you attend the annual parade, for example, bring some artifacts and decorations to the office that remind people of this event. When ethnic clients come in, make sure to talk about the holiday with them, wishing them good luck and good health as they leave.

170. *Be careful in using American idioms.* Someone learning the English language can be easily confused by many commonly used American phrases. Listen to yourself talk, and if you use an idiom, define it to make sure you have not made it more difficult for the client to understand you.

171. *Educate yourself about cultural taboos to avoid during transactions.* People from some cultures are offended if they are touched. Give extra information and itemized accounting of everything they have purchased and what they have paid. Watch carefully when customers conduct their shopping experiences. What do they do and say that can help you to respect their beliefs without condescending?

172. *Translate your signs, instructions and forms into appropriate languages.* This will help to make the business more accessible.

173. *When using paid advertising to attract ethnic groups, make doubly sure you are in touch with their cultural values.* Nothing could be more of a waste than to send out an advertising campaign that offends the very group whose trust you are trying to build. Test and retest slogans, graphic images and key words. Make sure that translations of your promotional materials are culturally appropriate as well as linguistically correct. Cultural translation takes into account values, taboos, perceptions of the dominant culture, and fears and anxieties about doing business with the dominant culture.

*P*rofiles Of *S*uccess

Chelsea Milling Company
Chelsea, Michigan

Business Profile: Producers of fine-milled wheat and corn flour and makers of the famous Jiffy biscuit and muffin mixes.

Word-of-Mouth Tactics: "We like to keep things simple here at Chelsea Milling," says Howdy Holmes, vice president of administration for the company. "We continually provide value to our customers in terms of the highest-quality ingredients at the best price in the nation," he says. Corporate marketing philosophy is not the only thing that is kept simple. The Jiffy biscuit and muffin mixes are also simple for consumers to use. Most Jiffy mixes require adding just one or two other ingredients.

A manufacturing firm, Chelsea Milling Company not only must focus on the consumers who take the product home, they must also maintain positive customer relations with food brokers and retailers. Long-term loyalty of this group is as valuable to the company as the loyalty of the end users. Just as the flour mixes offer value to consumers, Chelsea Milling's distribution and pricing policies offer value to wholesalers and retailers who are constantly trying to improve profitability in the very competitive food marketing industry.

Loyalty is maintained through consistent product quality, responsiveness in filling orders, education programs for brokers and retailers, and on-site guided tours of the mill. Retailers know that they can count on the food broker representatives to maintain the right mix and amount of product on the retail shelves. Every new account executive for the food brokers is given a guided tour of the factory. This builds and maintains word-of-mouth influence within the distribution channels.

Word of mouth is generated among the end users, too. Anyone who writes a good, bad or indifferent letter to Chelsea Milling receives a complimentary Jiffy gift mix. Every year thousands of consumers tour the factory to see firsthand the quality that is put into the product. Chelsea Milling is a national company, but it maintains a local presence by making donations to clubs and community organizations.

Results: Chelsea Milling Company has been able to maintain a leadership position in the food marketing industry for over 65 years. Parents who use Jiffy mixes pass on the tradition to their children, confirming the old saying that talk proceeds primarily along bloodlines. *(Used by permission from Chelsea Milling Company)*

Chapter **7**

---

*I*nfiltrating Industry Infrastructures

"An honest tale speeds best being plainly told."

— *Shakespeare*

"The invisible thing called a good name is made up of the breadth of numbers that speak well of you."

— *Lord Halifax*

*Y*our most important external marketing resource is the infrastructure of your industry. However, if you serve companies that make their homes in other industries, then the infrastructures of these other industries are your gold mines for word-of-mouth marketing.

For example, if your company is a law firm that specializes in serving plastics manufacturers and aluminum fabricators, you have two industries to mine for word-of-mouth referrals. A plastics factory serving aircraft manufacturers, home appliance manufacturers and automobile manufacturers has three gold mines to work. A bank serving the healthcare industry taps into the cadre of players who operate businesses in the healthcare industry.

Here's another example. You are an injection-molding plastics company serving midsized manufacturers. A sales representative comes into your office to show you a new computerized switching network that will not only control your plastic injection-molding equipment but will also calculate productivity, generate purchase orders for more raw materials, record and report on maintenance patterns for each machine, and generate client quality-improvement reports. In the course of the conversation, you are proud to mention that you just acquired a new molding machine that is twice as large as your others and will outperform any machine you have. The sales rep takes this bit of information and stores it away for future reference.

A few days later, this same sales rep is calling on a company that buys molded plastic parts to use in manufacturing aircraft equipment. She mentions the fact that she has just demonstrated her computer for your company and that you are seriously considering purchasing it. Then she says, "By the way, did you know they just bought a new injection-molding machine that will increase their capacity and double the size of the parts they can produce? They have an excellent quality-control program." Bingo. The manufacturer wants to know who this company is that has just tooled up with the latest technology. He wants a name and phone number. In a few days you get a telephone call that closes the word-of-mouth loop.

Like a system of superhighways, people, organizations and middle-men are the infrastructure that keep industry running smoothly. Word of mouth is often the mode of conducting business. Word-of-mouth tactics are a part of gathering information about the industry. Word of mouth generates truckloads of sales leads. Influence goes into motion primarily by word of mouth. Pricing policies are adjusted because of word of mouth. Stock prices go up or down on mere rumors. New-product developers use word of mouth to help them identify winning products. Word of mouth plays a key role in sourcing and purchasing raw materials, as well as in recruiting and hiring new employees. Word of mouth influences the financing decisions, the logistics and the distribution decisions of managers. The list can go on and on.

Building Strong Industry Relationships

Infrastructure word of mouth offers these advantages:

1. Many of the infrastructure leaders are also opinion leaders, marketing mavens or influentials. Not only do they influence your industry, they also influence people in other industries. A company's reputation can be spread outside the industry and then return with greater intensity.
2. When it is positive, word of mouth improves cooperation between companies within distribution channels. The key distribu-

tion intermediaries are more likely to support your company goals if they have heard positive things about you.

3. Word of mouth improves new-product acceptance. Positive word of mouth sets you up for getting an order from a distributor, a wholesaler or a retailer. They have limited space available to carry your product, but word of mouth can break through for you and be the difference between mere hope and success.

4. Word of mouth increases the likelihood that formal partnerships will evolve from loose, informal relationships. With positive word of mouth on your side, a beginning relationship can mature quickly into a formal bond that is difficult for competitors to break.

5. Word of mouth supports other promotion activities directed toward distribution channel members.

6. Infrastructure leaders are usually identifiable. Just look through the industry newsletters and magazines or the directories of professional associations and you will quickly find the names of the movers and shakers. These leaders can be found among the following:

   - Immediate past presidents
   - Current members of the board of directors, area or regional representatives
   - Association officers
   - Those honored for outstanding service to their organization
   - Committee chairpersons
   - Annual meeting planners
   - Representatives to the national or international organization
   - Liaisons with other groups like organized labor
   - Professional associations or government agencies
   - Innovators who have been profiled in journals
   - Attorneys
   - Insurance brokers
   - Temporary employment agencies
   - Nonprofit research groups that make it their business to know who's who
   - Professional trainers and motivational speakers

7. In industrial markets where a high degree of personal selling is needed to have the product gain acceptance, word of mouth is vital to success. Without a positive reputation,

- sales success is more difficult to achieve.
- it is more difficult to gain access to the decision makers.
- you have to spend more resources educating prospective clients about your services.

8. Buyers are increasingly more sophisticated. They want more objective information upon which to make purchase decisions. This is a great opportunity for your company, as these buyers are depending on the word of someone with personal experience.
9. Goodwill built up by word of mouth has a dampening influence on competitor aggressiveness. It makes it more difficult for your competitors to identify and sustain a unique competitive edge.

Notice this list's emphasis on relationships. Word of mouth happens because of relationships between the significant people in the industry. When you don't have a direct relationship with a target client, your existing business relationships carry your reputation through the social ties to others you don't know yet.

Challenges To Overcome

Don't assume that positive word of mouth is simple to achieve. Because of their complexity, industry infrastructures come with special challenges, too.

In industrial markets, the purchase decision is very complex. Typically, a formal process is required for making industrial purchases. Word of mouth can help with this, but it is not the only answer. It can take you days to identify the person who is crucial for your word-of-mouth marketing efforts.

Many people are involved in the purchase decisions of large organizations. Purchasing agents, department managers, supervisors, corporate presidents and vice presidents all play a role in decision making. This presents a real challenge to you as you attempt to build a reputation.

Some industry people you might at first consider important for word of mouth may be isolated from the consumers who buy your products. Their influence may be merely indirect.

Industrial buyers are increasingly specialized and hard to get to. It helps to have a positive reputation spread among the suppliers, but if these suppliers don't interact with *your* key customers, your reputation is the best-kept secret in the industry.

Purchasing agreements in some businesses tend to be long-term and difficult to break up. In spite of your winning ways and a spotless reputation, you may not get a chance at a new customer until your competitor's contract is up for renewal. Persist in your word-of-mouth program, because reputation is one of the chief reasons a customer decides to try a new company.

Brand loyalty to one of your competitors is difficult to overcome. But word of mouth is probably the most powerful wedge you can drive between a brand-loyal client and your competitor. It is the force that encourages brand-loyal clients to try your product just once.

Getting to Industry Movers and Shakers

The following infrastructure players may be found in most industries. Look through the Action Agenda list, and as you think of specific companies or individuals, write their names down. Your prospective clients ask these people for advice on whom to turn to for help. The opinion leaders among them will not only give information when asked, they will also offer unsolicited information about your company. These are the people who develop and spread your reputation.

*A*ction *A*genda

Cultivate these key contacts:

174. *Your own partners and managers.* Ideally, you can influence these individuals so that they promote your positive reputation. Practically, you should consider what effect each has on word of mouth. With whom does each have contact both inside and outside the industry? What is each doing to promote people talk?

175. *Professional associations.* Yes, it will pay you to join the professional association of some of your key clients. They have friends, some of whom are even their competitors, who need your services. Pick the geographic level of participation that makes the most sense (it is not necessary to network nationally if most of your potential clients come from one region).

176. Corporate executives who are linked in some way with potential clients. Every time you read a story of a corporate executive who has some tie with your target market, put his or her name on your card file of contacts. Write an introduction letter to these individuals. Send a postcard to let them know that you serve some of their friends. Pay a compliment to your clients when contacting these executives.

177. Designers and engineers. Designers and engineers, like attorneys, must keep up with the latest in technology, in top personnel and in operational methods. Their power lies not only in giving detailed (nonproprietary) information about your company to many others, but also in the fact that they are seen as experts in their fields. These specialists give speeches and are always looking for illustrations of positive growth to tell their audiences. Why not give them a few success stories to shout about to others? Offer to cross-promote with them (i.e., you will mention them to companies similar to yours and they will do likewise).

178. Other people involved with transactions with prospective clients. The next time you see your client, ask him or her to introduce you to some of these key people. Offer to do a small favor, inform them about your company and ask for referrals.

179. Suppliers of raw materials and technology. Organizations like these make it their business to know who can do what for their clients. If they can recommend your company with confidence, their own reputation will be enhanced. And when you can refer someone to them, they are likely to respond by sending you a customer.

180. Industry forecasters and futurists. To get noticed by one of these people requires that you become an innovator. It also helps to receive an appointment to an innovative think tank. Some of these individuals are so powerful, it pays to show them how you are innovating for the future. Bring them in for an educational seminar and then let them see your quality.

181. *Distributors and wholesalers.* The core of industry infrastructure, these organizations not only have their own influence, they also know many others who have influence. Get to know them and find out who they know.

182. *Sales organizations, brokers and agents.* Salespeople love to talk about the latest, the newest, the best. If you have them on your side, they can spread the word faster than anyone. What they need from you, of course, are some real-life examples of how their products or services are helping you make a lot of money. Start by identifying the salesmen and saleswomen who are regulars to your purchasing department. Get to know them personally. Ask them to talk with others about the good things they see in your firm. When you hear that they have put in a good word for you, thank them appropriately.

183. *Consultants and advisers.* Like designers and engineers, they make the rounds and enjoy talking about the latest things that are happening. Start with the people who advise you. Make sure they know the information you want others to know. Make a habit of inviting other consultants into your office to get acquainted. During these visits, give them information they can tell others.

184. *Writers, editors, publishers and reviewers.* Every industry has publications that serve as conduits for information. If your company has solved a major problem for a client, write a letter to the editor of the key magazine targeted to your client's industry. The purpose is not to toot your own horn but to feature your client and the success he or she has achieved with your help. Invite the writers and editors to your business for a tour. Relationships in this arena, like any other listed here, take time to develop. Be patient. Don't force yourself on those in the publishing world, but keep them informed. Then, when the opportunity comes to meet them, follow through.

185. *Advertising agencies and public relations firms.*   Like other service firms, advertising agencies like to see the latest promotional gadgets. They like to know when their work is successful. Start with the company that handles your advertising. Give them a lot more information about your business that they can share with potential customers. Call around to other advertising agencies to identify the ones that specialize in your clients' industries. Interview them—perhaps give them a chance to bid on a promotion project. Give them a load of information to share with their clients who are your potential customers.

186. *Government representatives, political leaders, regulators, members of commissions and agencies.*   These individuals must avoid being partial to any one company. In spite of this, they get opportunities to talk with many people linked with your potential clients. To build your business, get to know the officials who deal with your target clients.

187. *Trainers, motivational speakers, educators.*   Sometimes these individuals are also consultants. They are always looking for dynamic illustrations of how their ideas work for companies. Read their articles or listen to their speeches so you can learn what they get excited about. Then invite them in for a tour and show them how you are on the cutting edge of their great ideas. If they respond with enthusiasm, offer to let them use your company as an example in their speeches.

188. *Information research firms.*   Here is another example of companies to which prospective clients turn for advice. Personal relationships here can pay great dividends in referrals. Meet the key leaders and add them to your card file. Call them periodically and ask what is new in the industry.

189. *Financial intermediaries, escrow companies, financial planners, banks and turnaround specialists.*   This is an important group, because they have a high degree of contact with your prospective clients. It may pay you to change banking services in favor of a bank that specializes in your clients' industry. When they process loan applications or have discussions with their loyal customers, they have opportunities to refer to you.

190. Public interest groups, lobbying groups and watchdog groups. When you are on the good side of these types of groups, your reputation is spread quickly. Leaders in these organizations make it their business to give advice to others. They might as well be talking positively about you as about anyone else.

191. Executive search firms. Individuals in these companies usually have the ear of the top executives in companies you are trying to reach. Get on their good side and they will put in a good word for you when they visit their clients.

192. Any organization with which you have a long-term agreement. I recommend that you start with what is closest at hand and create success with those who know you best. You can be more direct with these organizations. Tell them how important your reputation is. Ask them if they are willing to make a referral to you. Then, when they follow through on their commitment, reward them appropriately.

193. Leasing companies. Here the key is identifying companies that lease equipment or services to your prospective clients. Offer to make referrals for them in exchange for their support.

194. Business brokers and appraisers. When these professionals close a deal, they are often asked by the new corporate owner for advice on where to turn for information or assistance. Even if they are not asked, they will offer the information if their client needs what you have and if they know you and trust you.

195. Lawyers. This is another type of professional to whom others turn for advice. Work at developing a relationship with one or two lawyers who serve prospective customers. Offer to refer them to others in exchange for their support.

196. *Select specific leaders and target them with carefully constructed information that they can pass on to others.* More people and organizations exist than you have time to actively encourage. Choose the leaders that make the most sense to you, and sustain your promotion efforts with these individuals. The most important information is personal experience in the good things you are doing for people, the dramatic success you are having, your consistent follow-through and your personality. Give them personal experience in these areas and they will have glowing things to say about you.

197. *Make every effort to arrange face-to-face meetings with leaders.* Supporting programs include telephone contact, letters and the media used by target clients. Take any chance you can get to meet with an infrastructure player, no matter how insignificant the stranger is to you.

198. *Actively seek opportunities to meet new movers and shakers.* Write them, telephone them or visit them to introduce yourself. Learn more about what they are all about, their goals, their dreams for the future. The same applies for new companies entering your industry. Remember that it is primarily people, and not companies, who spread your reputation.

199. *Communicate with opinion leaders before you send out your advertising.* When they receive your advertising, prospective clients are bound to ask one or more of these opinion leaders if they know you and if they have an opinion about what your service is like. Count on it. If you pretest your promotion pieces, conduct at least two tests: one with potential clients and one with infrastructure leaders.

200. *Maintain a constant stream of communication with leaders.* Keep them informed of the latest developments, new technology, new processes, new personnel and new materials. To do an effective job for you, these individuals need current information to tell others. Give it to them. I recommend a series of personal letters that give them news and commentary. Formal newsletters can work, too.

201. Host key decision makers for a briefing.   An industry or government update makes an excellent theme to use. A catered meal adds a classy touch. Or, host such a meeting in a banquet room.

202. Develop relationships with suppliers other than those on your roster, even if you don't buy from them.   Why? First, these suppliers can make referrals to you in hopes of getting your business. If you do get a referral, do your best to purchase supplies from the referring company unless such an action violates antitrust laws or jeopardizes your current long-term relationships. Second, you may need them if you have to switch suppliers in a hurry.

203. Become a highly visible promoter of cooperation and collaboration among members of the industry.   Smoothly running logistics for procurement, shipping, receiving, storing and distributing raw materials and supplies, and distributing products to consumers are evidence that this cooperation is present.

204. Sustain performance of word of mouth to see the effects of your work in the industry.   Hit-or-miss efforts will require more time to generate results. If you have time for just a modest program, make it work consistently.

205. Identify key referral agents who have brought you business in the past.   Do something to thank them for their trust in you. Analyze this group. Ask yourself, "Who are the other people similar to these that I should meet?"

Chapter 8

*F*inding More Champion Customers in Your Community

"A man's good deeds are known only at home, his bad deeds far away."

— Chinese proverb

"Your best salesman is a satisfied customer."

— Traditional American business proverb

I have emphasized the importance of developing strong relationships with champion customers and referral sources. Now I'm going to ask you to take those principles one step further and use the power of networking in community groups with the help of your champion customers. Although this chapter focuses on networking with organized groups, all your word-of-mouth marketing can be seen as a form of networking.

Every community has a network of powerful communication grapevines. These channels of energy are used to do more than pass gossip; they are a popular means of getting things done. If you want to have a strong ally in building your reputation, tap into the community grapevine. Opinion leaders often give, withhold, distort, clarify, confirm, evaluate and edit information about people and events. If the right person gets positive information about you, the news will travel like a grass fire in a windstorm. Negative news travels even faster.

Your public relations task is to link with both the formal and informal connections your customers have with other people in the community, many of whom fit the champion profile. However, many business owners fail to create a synergy between the rest of their reputation-building work and public relations with community groups. It is as if the two were totally unrelated, when in fact they are brother and sister.

Community groups can be some of the most productive in transmitting your reputation. Unless you are involved with some of these highly effective grapevines, you will be a mystery to the community around you. People will not know very much about you, but they will still form an opinion about what you are like. This could be bad or good. Why take a chance?

If you are able to overwhelm a few champion customers with excellent service, the news of your work will get out in the groups they belong to. By the time the message gets passed to the third or fourth person down the grapevine, it may be slightly altered, but chances are that it will still be positive. It may even be embellished by well-meaning people who listen to your champion talk and then make the report sound even better to the next person. In the process, people are getting to know you whether you like it or not. You are building your business the old-fashioned way—through your reputation.

People who are isolated aspire to be part of a group and are likely to be influenced by spokespersons of these "aspirational" groups. In your business, place signals to these individuals that you are a part of their aspirational group. If you become a spokesman for the group, make that known to your clients.

Groups To Look For

There are various kinds of groups in every community. One type of group consists of the informal friendships between people at a similar stage in life or with similar vocational or avocational interests. A group of young mothers taking turns baby-sitting for each other, a group of men who go on a quarterly fishing trip and the relationship between private pilots who fly for relaxation are examples of informal friendships. All may represent opportunities for your organization.

Another type is the formal membership group that comes together to help its members achieve a common goal. Examples include the local amateur radio club, the philanthropy group at the community hospital, the women's auxiliary of the university and the downtown business association.

An open group is one that is loosely structured and allows people to drift in and out without making a commitment. This is the case with the people who seem to end up together at the local baseball park on summer nights to cheer on the home team and those who take part in semiannual walk-a-thons and races that benefit a local charity.

Other groups are closed and membership is closely controlled. More stable membership exists in closed groups, because the people know each other better and they make formal commitments to support group goals. Closed groups include organizations such as membership-by-invitation service clubs, the employees from the nearby factory and the local church's board of directors.

It is not necessary to precisely categorize each group in the community, because many groups fit into more than one category. What is important, however, is to begin looking for opportunities to tap into the power of these groups through your customers and their relationships with group members.

Why People Join Groups

Groups fulfill several needs for customers. For example, they provide a sense of belonging. When customers attend group meetings and get involved in group functions, they focus on the people around them instead of on themselves. Group meetings are structured settings for communication with others. Even if formal "group business" is conducted at a group meeting, there is always informal social interaction before, during and after the meeting. When your customers participate in groups, they have an opportunity to learn and practice new roles modeled by others. They learn what is culturally acceptable and test the limits of acceptability by asking questions, observing behavior and making comments. Groups help people grow and change. The members of a group have a common purpose or function when they work together. Finally, groups provide a setting in which things can be done together.

Group communication affects everyone in the group. When customers attend group meetings, their attitudes are shaped unconsciously. They develop enduring values and specific opinions about a variety of issues. There is so much power in group communications that sometimes group members or their friends will act on a suggestion because of where it came from rather than critically evaluating its content. A few high-visibility leaders in a group can, through their charismatic way with people, sway opinions on a variety of subjects, including products and services in your industry.

How To Pick a Community Group

Almost every book on public relations for business owners suggests that someone in the company get involved with a few social groups in the community. While I don't disagree with this, I recommend that you analyze carefully which groups are the best ones to get involved with. There may be many groups with which you will have brief contact, but you will probably choose to become a member of only a few.

The local library or chamber of commerce has a printed list of the various community groups in the area. As you read the list, think of the types of customers your business attracts: Are you looking for children and their parents, adults with specific product interests or people in a certain social class? If you are not sure what types of groups your favorite customers belong to, look through your records and create a profile of the typical customer and customer family. Start asking these typical customers what groups they belong to or what groups they want to belong to. Make a note of the groups in which your customers hold formal or informal membership. Are these the types of groups you or your spouse could join? Are they the types of groups you would be glad to support with your volunteer time, attendance and donations? Remember that informal groups are usually not listed in official directories.

There are two marketing strategies to choose between when one is thinking about community groups. The first is the strategy of maximizing the contacts you already have, because you have happy customers holding membership in these groups. The second is the strategy of expanding your reach by getting involved with new groups. The champion-type people in those new groups will help you tap the resources of other grapevines.

Whatever strategy you select, stay with it long enough to see whether it is working. Six to nine months is the average minimum time needed to scope out the opportunities and determine whether your networking efforts are paying off. But be patient. Networking results may not be seen until the second or third year of group participation.

Your constant challenge in networking is identifying and working with opinion leaders. Because you are a business professional, group leaders are likely to ask your opinions and ideas. They will respect your background and experience even if they know nothing about how you treat customers. When this happens, do as the ancient proverb suggests: Count others better than yourself. If you do, the group leaders will talk about you to others.

Working with a Variety of Groups

You won't have time to get involved with every type of community group. In addition, you have your own interests to consider. Long-term involvement with a group suggests that you get enjoyment from the process. If you are not a joiner, there are still opportunities to tap the power of word of mouth in groups. Here are a few suggestions.

*A*ction *A*genda

Cultivate these social groups:

206. *Women's groups.*   Women are the leading decision makers in products like food, clothing and healthcare. They are usually the ones who decide when to take a sick child to the doctor, what clothing to buy for their families and what will be on the menu for dinner. Because of their shopping experience, women are experts in selecting products and personal services. They know about waiting, scheduling and paying for services. Listen to what they say and you will learn how your reputation can be enhanced.

In each community there are usually several women's groups, most of which will welcome an expert speaking on an issue that is important to them. Contact the local library or university to find out which groups are in your area. Compare this list with the groups your female customers belong to. Assign an employee to offer to speak to a women's group on a topic relevant to your industry. Let your customer/members suggest whom to talk with to make the arrangements or let them talk with the leaders directly. If you involve a champion customer in the process, you will get much more word of mouth about that speaking event.

Besides the organized groups they belong to, many women also have informal communication networks that can contribute to your reputation.

207. *Employer groups.*   Some businesses have tapped successfully into the working groups in the community. Lunchtime brown-bag lecture series work in some companies. Helping a company design a personal finance program and then giving financial education lectures as part of the program is an example of how one financial planner networks in her community.

You can also tap into the power of the corporate grapevine by letting your champion customers speak for you. Make a list of the major companies your customers work for. Ask the champion customers if there is a company newsletter. Ask them how you can communicate to other workers what your company does. Examples include putting up personal notices on the company bulletin board. You can contact businesses yourself but probably will not be allowed to put up a notice that you are accepting new customers. Your champion customers have the clout to get that done for you, so let them try.

208. *Middle management and technicians.*   When I give lectures on word-of-mouth marketing, I suggest that people interested in tapping into the power of the grapevine should start with what is most natural in their line of work. The single most important action you can take to enhance word-of-mouth marketing is to be congenial toward managers you work with. In many ways they can be your greatest supporters, and they will send you a lot of customers.

A seminar series that you conduct just for technical experts will enhance their perception of your competence. Pick topics that are interesting to them or that relate directly to making their work more productive. Keep the seminars short and, above all, practical. Seminars are a great way for you to get to know these employees better as people. It will change the way you deal with them in the customer service area.

209. *Seniors.*   Seniors have the most experience shopping and buying products and services. They have an enormous influence over their families. Opinion leader seniors are also at the time of life when they can be honest and direct, and are often looked up to for advice. For all these reasons, you should tap into the powerful energy of word-of-mouth marketing among seniors.

A variety of senior groups exist, many of which enjoy having a business owner give a speech on a consumer product topic in which they are interested. They enjoy asking questions and getting your opinions on the latest products and services they hear about on the news. Seniors are quick to relate experiences they have had. This, too, is good for your reputation. Someday they will be talking up your business to someone else.

Interacting with seniors may require patience. You are in a hurry; they have all the time in the world. You don't want to hear about what happened to their daughter-in-law on her recent cruise; they want to tell you about someone important to them, someone who could be a prospective customer. As a word-of-mouth marketing specialist, I say, "Yes, you do want to hear about these things. These conversations can be rewarding in themselves and give you a chance to develop relationships with champions."

If you become active in a senior organization, the word will spread like wildfire. "Did you know that Ms. _____ is a member of our group? She is such a nice woman" will be the type of thing they say. They appreciate the few business owners who take the time to get involved with seniors' groups at the grass-roots level.

210. *Social and service clubs.* A business owner recently told me that he thought it was a waste of time to go to the local chapter of the international service club in his area: "I attended a few meetings, and I got frustrated at all the mindless bull that was going on there. I have better things to do than go to lunches all the time." Not everyone sees the value in actively participating in service clubs or chambers of commerce. It has to be something you enjoy or your dissatisfaction will quickly show.

Service clubs have a structured hierarchy of leadership. Respect this hierarchy at all costs as you begin networking. It is acceptable to let the person responsible for planning programs know you are available to speak on one or more topics. If you decide to be innovative with business etiquette, be cautious and be sure to follow the formal and informal rules of that particular group. If you ask your champion customers which groups they belong to, you will have a short list of the key groups with which you should begin networking. The next time a champion customer comes into the office for services, let that customer know you have contemplated joining the same group and want to know what he or she thinks about it. What is involved in membership in the group? Ask these questions only after investigating your options and narrowing the field to the commitments you can keep. Why should you tell a champion customer that you are interested in his or her group? It starts the word-of-mouth marketing within that group immediately.

211. *Neighborhood associations.*   If you want to find a group of opinion leaders gathered together in one place, attend a local neighborhood homeowners' association. The people who attend are the ones to whom others listen. You may have to endure a lot of political intrigue, but this is one of the best groups to use to tap into the grapevine of word of mouth. Offer to work on a subcommittee or help plan the annual barbecue in the park. Personal involvement on a consistent basis is the key to success.

212. *Identify your customers' involvement with groups.*   A personal conversation with your customers will often reveal a lot about their links with social groups. Here are some questions to get customers talking about their experiences with groups.

- Do you belong to any clubs or organizations?
- What does your group do?
- Tell me about your group.
- How long have you been a member? (Newer members are still learning the ropes and are typically farther away from those who hold the most influence.)
- Do you get involved with helping people in the group?
- Do you hold an office?

Ask only the questions you feel are appropriate. You don't want to interrogate your customer with a lot of personal questions. On your list of champion customers, make notes to remind yourself of group affiliations. Don't trust your memory.

213. ***Make contact with groups your customers belong to.*** When you attend a group meeting, introduce yourself to the people who appear to be the leaders. Look for the champion customer and say hello. Let him or her introduce you to others he or she considers important. Conduct careful observation to determine which people seem to be the focal points of conversation. Who receives the most questions? With whom do people gather before and after the meeting?

214. ***Make a small donation of time, money or other resources to the group you intend to stay with.*** Remember that groups understand the importance of reciprocity. If you give something too big, you may get only a symbolic gift in return, something that will not help you build your practice. Avoid making pit stops at groups you have no interest in coming back to unless it is in response to a request by one of your champion customers.

215. ***Avoid making an ostentatious splash into the group.*** It is much better to get involved at the pace the group sets for you through its activities. Splashy entrances can smack of commercial interest and raise suspicions about your motives. It is much better to get genuinely involved with group activities and help the members with their problems. What you are after here is to build your reputation, not merely grab a few customers. If you help the group even though you have nothing to gain by it, they will reciprocate after trust has been built.

216. ***Come early or stay late at group meetings.*** These are the most important times for networking. If you swing in at the last minute and then leave early because you have other things to do, you won't get much sympathy from those who are at the meeting, and you probably won't get much accomplished in terms of marketing. If you are chronically late, you will have little opportunity to acknowledge the champion customers you see there. You will be looked upon as someone not completely involved in the group and may be treated as an outsider for a long time.

It is the social time before and after the meeting when the most important group work occurs. It is also during this time that you can have the greatest impact through personal conversation. Before and after the meeting, you can build bridges for later referrals. Don't expect to get referrals immediately, but do follow up on any promise you make to the people you meet there. If you fail to follow up as they expect, negative word of mouth may result. If you must choose between coming late and leaving early, study the group to see where most of the informal networking occurs. If most people let their hair down after the formal session, make sure to stay late. If the social hour seems to occur before the formal meeting, get there early.

217. *Respect the chain of command in the group.* If you are too aggressive in trying to communicate with those who hold the power in the group, you could be shut out before you even get started. Groups are sensitive about following protocol and the unwritten rules of how things work. Be careful to honor the accepted communication patterns.

218. *Clarify their expectations and fulfill your promises.* If you are asked by the group's program planner to give a speech, find out the expectations before you deliver the speech. What type of presentation has met with the most enthusiasm in the past? How much time are you expected to use? Do many of the members have to go to other meetings after the program? Do they like to have time for questions after the speech? When you have clear expectations, stick to your promises. If the meeting is supposed to end at 1 PM, sit down at 12:55 to let the chairperson wrap things up.

219. *Carry your business cards with you.* Don't flaunt them, but have them ready.

220. *Form relationships that will last.* Focus on getting to know a few people rather than flitting from person to person and developing a relationship with no one. If a group leader's personality irritates you, you don't have to become friends with that person. Getting to know that person, however, will pay off later if he or she is one of the opinion leaders.

Profiles Of Success

Pete's Plumbing
Long Beach, California

Business Profile: Pete's Plumbing offers a full range of heating, plumbing and drain-cleaning services for residential property.

Word-of-Mouth Tactics: Patti Hillis, company manager, says that the company tries to build word of mouth by building repeat business from an established base of loyal customers. The company carefully cultivates relationships with investment property owners who count on the plumbers to respond within an hour or two for routine service calls and even faster in emergencies.

In newspaper advertising and in new-customer welcome letters, she emphasizes that most of the company's customers are "re-pete" customers. To create a silent testimonial, she sends letters notifying neighbors that a Pete's Plumbing customer has just purchased a major plumbing project on the block. The letter invites the neighbors to become preferred "re-pete" customers. The campaign is designed to have the same effect as that achieved when the company service truck is parked in the neighborhood. To find the names and addresses of neighbors, she uses a telephone company street address directory (sometimes called a criss-cross directory) that lists by street name the house numbers and names of residents. When she identifies a specific name of a current customer who refers business their way, she always sends a thank-you letter.

For a contractor like Pete's Plumbing, relationships with other trade professionals generate referrals, too. And Patti maintains relationships with a variety of other contracting companies that send her referrals. She responds by sending them referrals and by verbally acknowledging their support.

Service staff are trained to be aware of customer fears that the job won't be finished in a timely manner and that the plumber might leave a mess behind. Customers are kept informed about work schedules. If any unusual circumstances are encountered, the customer is informed immediately. Finally, the plumber always cleans up afterward. No matter what the property looked like when he arrived, it always looks as good or better when the plumber leaves.

Once a real estate broker called Patti in an emergency. Impressed at the responsiveness that Pete's Plumbing provided, the broker now asks the company to service most of the plumbing problems he encounters.

Results: Eighty percent of all service calls are from repeat customers. This is an accomplishment that speaks of the consistent service Pete's Plumbing offers. Word of mouth is second only to the company's modest Yellow Page advertisement in drawing new customers. *(Used by permission from Pete's Plumbing)*

Chapter 9

*I*ntroducing New Products and Services

"Everyone talks of what he loves."

— *Thomas Fuller*

*I*ntroducing new products and services into the market can mean the difference between mediocre existence and exciting growth. As you look at your current products, be aware that in a few years the market will change enough to require changes in what you offer your customers. In most businesses, new-product development is the life-blood of staying close to the market. It is the way you stay ahead of the competition. It is also the way you can continue growing. If your industry experiences swings in demand for your services or products, offering new products can smooth out demand, making cash flow much more predictable and your life more enjoyable. Creating new products helps you spread your risks, attract new clients, build your capital reserves, increase your efficiency with your current marketing relationships and expand your ability to serve others. It also offers new opportunities to increase profitability.

One important element needed to introduce a new product or service is advertising. Without some type of advertising, most new products will not get off the ground. Advertising gets your message out to larger numbers of people faster than word of mouth can. Paid promotion stimulates demand, generates inquiries and gives prospective clients important information to use in their purchase decision process. While I recognize the importance of advertising for new product introduction, I suggest that you make your paid promotional tactics a complement to your word-of-mouth program instead of the reverse.

Many advertising experts will counsel you to advertise and let word of mouth take care of itself. When these advisers get hold of your marketing program, they can make word of mouth alien to their own pet ideas—ignored, taken for granted and robbed of its true power to help you succeed. I think this is wrong for several reasons.

Beginning with word of mouth gets you close to clients in a way that beginning with advertising will not. I've seen thousands of advertising dollars blown into oblivion simply because the business professional was not close enough to opinion leaders in the market to understand the subtleties of their current clients or prospective clients. A word-of-mouth program forces you to test the key messages, the key benefits and the important features of the new service with opinion leaders. If you do this before you generate a lot of expensive advertising, you will minimize your risks of financial waste and improve your chances of getting a good return on your advertising investment.

Engaging in a word-of-mouth program will get you close to clients in a way that market research will not. Opinion surveys, focus groups and secondary research all can be helpful. Very few successful new products are introduced without conducting research. The first challenge in conducting research is to find enough money to pay for what you are told you need. The second challenge is to find a use for it once you have paid for it. If you engage in a word-of-mouth marketing program, you will get the benefits from the research you do as well as from the promotional value it brings to your company.

If you start with paid advertising, the messages potential clients get about you from word of mouth may be inconsistent with what they get from your advertising. Here the risk is in creating confusion for your clients. They hear one thing about you from opinion leaders and see another thing in your paid promotion. If this happens, your advertising may do more harm than good.

Word of mouth has just as much power as paid promotion. Never under estimate the power that a small group of hand-picked champions have for spreading the word to qualified prospective clients. For some products, word of mouth has much more power than advertising in influencing a consumer to switch brands or to try a new product.

Paid advertising will inform consumers, while word of mouth will influence them to act.

If you fly an advertising campaign without including your champions, they will be dumfounded when they are asked for their opinion about the new service. While they may have some nice things to say about your other services, their lack of firsthand knowledge of your new product can slow the decision process for the new client. If you begin with your champions—informing them, encouraging them, rewarding them for their hard work—they will have even better results when your paid advertising hits the streets. Remember the role that champions play in the decision process: They help shape attitudes just before a person decides whether to call you for an appointment.

Instead of making your champions last on the list for promotion, make them first. If you do, you will get closer to the market; you will conduct the type of meaningful research that will actually help you do something; and you will minimize the risk of creating a communication nightmare. Test your communication with champions, test your new services with champions and test your assumptions about the market with champions. If you do this, you will set yourself up for success.

When Brazilian coffee was introduced into Romania, Romanian coffee consumption was approximately two cups of coffee per person per week. Before any advertising was developed for the product, distributors engineered a campaign of giving coffee samples to opinion leaders in every major city. In just one year, coffee consumption was up to approximately seven cups of coffee per person per week. Word of mouth has tremendous leverage to change consumer behavior toward new products.

What Influences the Success of New Products?

It is not sheer volume of advertising that makes or breaks the success of new products. It is a combination of things, all of which are inseparable from word of mouth. According to the experts, there are several key influences on success. The first is a unique selling advantage as compared with competitors or with the consumer's perception of problems and possible solutions. The more unique the product or its benefits, the more likely it is that word of mouth will be spread. However, if the product is difficult for consumers to differentiate, word of mouth will be less likely.

The second key influence is whether the product matches the values prized by consumers. At the core of values are shared cultural beliefs and attitudes. A new product that violates these core values will have a much more difficult time gaining acceptance among consumers in a cultural group that is offended. Not only must the product match well with consumer values, but the promotion methods, pricing policies and distribution tactics must also be compatible with consumers' behavior. The more closely a product is aligned with core cultural values, the more likely it is that word of mouth will promote sales.

How complex the product or service is for the consumer to use is the third key influence. Highly complex products have a more difficult time getting established than do simple products. An exception to this rule is the new table and floor games, which are highly complex. The complexity of these games is one of their advantages.

The fourth key influence is whether the product can be tested by consumers before they make their purchase decision. Free trial offers, lease-to-own arrangements, test drives and in-store demonstrations are examples of allowing consumers to test a product before they buy. Prepurchase trials usually enhance positive word of mouth if the use of the product meets with approval.

The final key influence concerns how easy it is to communicate to consumers what the product is and how it benefits them. Here is another area in which word of mouth plays an important role. When satisfied opinion leaders talk about your product to others, they must be able to describe in a conversation what you cannot describe in a headline or 30 seconds on the radio.

By itself, word-of-mouth promotion tactic is a strong influence. It is personal influence that spreads the news about a successful product from the originator to those who use it.

How New Products Gain Acceptance

Research from a variety of fields shows how innovations spread from a starting point to acceptance in a large population. For example, researchers have found that it is primarily social channels of communication that carry news about a new product from innovator to early adopters, and then to later adopters. These early adopters share characteristics similar to those described in Chapter 3. They are innovative, have a high degree of contact with others, actively look for information on innovations and are looked to for advice on new products. Until enough of these early adopters have experience with the product, the word-of-mouth network can be dormant.

Research has also taught marketers that it takes time for an innovation to spread through a population. Pricing policies, distribution planning, product quality and promotion tactics (including word of mouth) all play an important role in the length of time needed to achieve the product's acceptance. When critical mass is reached for successful buyers to experience the product and to talk about their experience, then the diffusion process snowballs and grows rapidly.

Diffusion of an innovation will not necessarily reach an entire population. However, we say diffusion is complete when it has saturated to the maximum level possible in one segment of the population. Diffusion also can repeat in other segments or at a later time when existing, mature products are revived.

How To Develop New Products

While the process may differ slightly from one business to another, the seven general principles below may be used as a guide. Notice that in several of the steps word of mouth is important.

1. *Idea generation.* Many innovative ideas come to business executives who listen to their champion customers talk. Whether you conduct formal focus groups or informal interviews with key champions, you will be initiating word of mouth. This is the perfect time to brainstorm with some of your champions. Spend time talking with them about the changes they see coming in your industry. Ask them their hopes and fears for the future. During the idea-generation stage, the goal is to gather as many ideas as possible. Don't be concerned about their practicality; you will have a chance later to eliminate ideas that won't work.

2. *Idea screening.* This is where you ask the following questions: Does the concept match well with our corporate direction and our existing products? Which of the new product ideas can be supported by our current reputation? Which products will cause confusion among our champion clients? Which product ideas are the most consistent with our position in the market as defined by the publics we serve and the clients who are loyal to us?

3. *Concept testing.* During this phase of new product development you have another great opportunity to interact with opinion leaders. In concept testing, you verbally describe your new product concept and get their feedback on how it would best work for them. Ask them about pricing, distribution, benefits and many other issues. Ask them about company reputation and how well the new ideas match with your position in the market. Concept testing should be completed in an environment where customers feel free to be honest. This is usually accomplished by using an independent focus group facilitator. When conducting focus groups, you may want to gather information from both opinion leaders and potential customers. After completing this phase, you will have some initial assumptions about the most appropriate marketing strategies to follow.

4. *Business analysis.* Now that you have generated a long list of product ideas, screened them for their "fit" with your company and eliminated inappropriate ideas based on the concept testing, your goal is to determine whether the remaining product ideas will be profitable. Here is where you make your first estimates on unit costs of production, break-even volumes needed, expected demand and sales projections (for first-time sales, repeat sales and replacement sales), and estimating the long-term cash flow of the new product.

5. *Prototype development.* If your product idea passes the business analysis tests, you should develop a fully functional product sample before trying to take it to opinion leaders. Why? You don't want them talking more about the bugs you had to work out of the product than about its benefits. During this phase you will test your prototype with real consumers, including opinion leaders, to determine their preferences and their opinions about the new product. This is usually done by giving away samples in exchange for their feedback on written questionnaires such as rating scales.

Your goal during this phase is to make sufficient product refinements to achieve a high level of product performance and a high level of consumer satisfaction.

6. *Test marketing.* At this point you will have established a brand name, the packaging and the initial communications themes. Now you need to see how your new product does in real-life market dynamics. This is also the point at which you risk more money (to produce the first run of the product, establish the product in the distribution system and pay for the first communications to the target market). If you forget the opinion leaders at this phase, you will stand to miss a great opportunity to increase sales. In a test market, you want to see customers *try* the product the first time as well as become repeat purchasers. You are also testing the distribution system, merchandising strategies and communication tactics. After the bugs have been worked out, you need to involve your champions in the test phase. Will your loyal customers buy? Will those who already trust you make a purchase commitment? I recommend test marketing with champions first for the following reasons:

- They are already loyal to you and are more forgiving if errors crop up. In addition, they will tell you how to make the product better.
- If the product is a success, they will begin telling others immediately.
- Their feedback will help you refine your paid advertising program to reach out to those who don't know you the same way they do. They will know by experience the chief benefits that will get the most attention. Their opinion on the price will help you refine your pricing tactics. They will have suggestions for improving the product itself.
- They will recommend the best type of client to target.

7. *Rolling it out.* Assuming the test market phase is successful, now you decide how to expand the marketing program. Some companies miss the opportunity to use the power of opinion leaders in the rush of communicating with large groups. I recommend that you build a paid promotion program around the work of opinion leaders. Make it consistent with what opinion leaders are saying to others. Use examples of opinion leaders in your advertising.

(More examples on this point can be found at the end of this chapter and in Chapter 10.)

Cross-Selling

Although this may be seen as one of the tactics to introduce a new product or service, I highlight it separately because of its special power to generate sales. Cross-selling is the process of offering new products or services to your current clients. These services may not necessarily be unique in the market; they may merely be new to your company. In any case, cross-selling is your attempt to get current clients to buy something new from you.

Think of the marketing leverage you have here. If it takes $100 to capture a new customer but only $10 to get that customer to buy something new from you after he or she has already come to trust you, wouldn't you want to use that kind of marketing power? I would. And businesses that successfully launch new products use this power through cross-selling to loyal customers.

This is how it works. You have a group of people who are your supporters. These people have had positive experiences with your products. Then along comes your great idea for a new product. It can be a product new to your company or a truly unique product. Your first step is to communicate with current customers that you have a new product available. This can be done using point-of-purchase displays or sales scripts. It also can be accomplished using direct mail or a scripted telephone marketing campaign. Be sure you include a clear method and reason for loyal customers to respond (response cards, special offers with time limits, special pricing policies for first trials, guarantees, etc.). You carefully track your sales success with the target loyal consumers. You track how many opinion leaders make purchases. Finally, you introduce a program to encourage opinion leaders to spread the new product's reputation to others.

Brand Image Issues

Brand image development is a two-edged sword. On the one hand, word of mouth is one of the surest ways to protect your product from competitors who will plunder your market share. Your good reputation is about the only thing competitors cannot steal. As competitors surface with "me-too" products, you can encourage loyalty by helping your customers extend the life or use of your product. You can emphasize the quality in your product, which has been tested by many satisfied customers. And you can increase the level of before-sale and after-sale service you provide. While it is probably costing your competitors more cash for paid advertising to win customers away from your reputation, you cannot just sit by and be casually unresponsive. You may have to make product revisions, change your distribution channel relationships to add value for customers, increase your paid advertising, refine your brand image or change your pricing policies. All of these will cost money to implement. However, without the solid base of positive word of mouth working for you, these defensive tactics will cost you even more.

In a competitive situation, customers must be able to differentiate your product from others. If the brand image is not well defined, even if it is positive, potential customers will probably ignore it.

On the other hand, you can bring a new product into a saturated market dominated by weaker products. Through brand image development you can use the power of word of mouth to win new customers. Here are some ideas on how to make this happen.

*A*ction *A*genda

221. *Let customers use your product in their work setting first.* Their experience at work will carry over into their purchase decisions for their personal life. To accomplish this, your distribution efforts will be focused on the organizational markets first, many of which buy in large quantities. While your competitors spend wildly to attract the attention of the masses, you can quietly introduce new customers to your product.

222. *Compare and contrast.* When a competitor makes a change in perceived quality or in ingredients, show customers how this changes the competitor's position. Make a comparison chart you can show marketing mavens and product enthusiasts.

223. *Let them try it out for free.*   Give product samples or loans of your product to let customers actually experience the difference for themselves.

224. *Be consistent.*   Develop a clear, consistent image for your product through the use of graphic images, type fonts, slogans, colors and labels. You have to spend some money on these items anyway, so make them consistent and make them strong communicators for your product's developing reputation.

225. *Start with known opinion leaders in your community.*   These individuals can be current clients who have purchased other products from you in the past, or they can be nonclients who are well connected with the types of clients you believe will be interested in the new product.

226. *Educate.*   Conduct educational seminars for community opinion leaders and introduce your new product in this setting. When you do so, give plenty of detailed information to evaluate and digest. Prepare a written handout to give to participants. Political leaders often use an appropriate community forum to disclose new programs relating to those in attendance. They know that this works in spreading word of mouth.

227. *Use the rule of five.*   Make sure you give at least three to five exposures of your message to opinion leaders via a variety of methods, such as direct marketing, personal selling, public relations and news stories. Unless the minimum number of exposures is achieved, your message will probably not get through. This principle applies as much to communicating with opinion leaders as it does to paid promotion directed toward the general public or a group of prospective clients.

228. *Identify the news angle and educate the press.*   Get a feature story in the newspaper about one of your champions using your new service. Feature stories work well when they include some kind of photo opportunity, a remarkable achievement or a significant change in the way your client interacts with his or her customers or the public—something that has real news value. You can't control when feature stories will be run by a newspaper. But when you succeed in getting a story placed, you will benefit in dozens of ways:

- Your credibility increases among those who don't even know you yet.
- Prospective clients tune into the core issues your champion experienced—they empathize.
- Most feature stories have word-of-mouth potential in them simply because they are a story. And people like to tell stories to other people.

229. *Plant a story.*   Planting a story involves the following steps:

- Start with a simple phone call to the editor, asking him or her to review your story. Don't expect a commitment to use the material. All you can accomplish here is for the editor to notice your material.
- If your story has an unusual photographic opportunity, make your first call to the chief of photography at the publication. Remember that his or her primary interest is in getting a good photograph and not in the details of the story.
- Write a pitch letter to the newspaper or magazine editor outlining how this service event is significant to a wide public.
- Include a news release summarizing the details in succinct fashion. If the editor is interested, he or she will call you for more details. If the editor is serious about publishing a story, he or she will set up an appointment for an interview and a photo session with you and your client.
- Make a short follow-up phone call to the editor to determine if what you sent is useful. If the editor wants to discuss the material on the telephone, she or he will tell you so. Don't ask to discuss the story on the telephone. And don't assume that because the editor received the material and was willing to acknowledge receiving it, he or she is interested in printing a story about it.
- Even if the editor expresses interest, don't assume that you will get anything in print. Local, regional and national news will take precedence over a feature story anytime. The editor can have a sudden change of mind for any reason. If the publication does not use the material, let it go. Do not, under any circumstances,

call the editor for an explanation. Doing this will kill your chances for a later story.

230. *Offer your new service or product as a premium add-on to someone else's product or service.* Visit a well-respected business that is known to attract clientele similar to your target market. Offer your new product (at a big discount) as a premium add-on to something they already successfully sell. Why would you want to do this? To get their opinion leaders talking about your product.

231. *Cross-promote with other organizations.* Use co-op discount coupons or special deal invitations (make style consistent with target champions) with another (related) business. The other business gives out the coupons to its champion customers. You do the same for the other business.

232. *Collaborate with others in your educational efforts.* Cohost an educational seminar with another company that has champions with interests similar to your new product. This way you will have two groups of champions who can talk about your new product instead of one. For example, a real estate broker and a financial planner; an accountant and an attorney; an interior decorator and a remodeler.

233. *Be your next best sales rep.* Satisfied customers are your best, but use direct sales to known champions convincing them of the benefits and asking for their support in referring others to you. This is an opportunity that is often lost simply because companies do not ask opinion leaders for their help. A simple letter with a special gift offer works in many businesses.

234. *Use personal letters.* Write a personal letter to community leaders whether they are your customers or not. Follow up the letter with a call explaining why you sent the piece to them. Tell them that you wanted them to know about your new service; and if they ever come across someone who needs this type of service, ask if they would think about referring that person to you.

235. *Cross-sell.* Cross-sell every new client who comes to buy an existing service. Instruct your staff to mention the new product or service on the telephone, at the reception desk and in the consultation room.

236. *Set up a frequent-referral program.* When champions refer a certain number of others for the new service, gladly refund the money they spend on the service, or give them something of value for their efforts.

237. *Go on a story-telling binge.* Tell why customers wanted the product, how the product got started—all the human interest elements. Stories are a powerful medium in which word of mouth gets passed from one person to another. Encourage your employees to tell stories. Encourage your champion customers to tell their own stories.

238. *Collect testimonials from customers.* If you are slow getting testimonials, ask for them from your happiest clients. Get permission from satisfied clients to use them as a reference for prospective clients who have questions or doubts.

239. *Use your customer's existing knowledge as leverage for the new product.* In your paid promotion efforts, associate your new service or product with existing services and products that you offer or that your target champions already know about through positive personal experience. This positioning tactic has worked thousands of times.

240. *Make visible your client list or referral list.* If you get telephone inquiries, develop a short script incorporating the names of a few high-visibility clients or referring professionals who trust you. If potential clients come to your office to purchase, post the list of clients and referring professionals in a visible place in the lobby or in a prominent place. If you send information in the mail to potential clients, include your most credible referral sources and satisfied clients in your promotional materials.

241. Combine your word-of-mouth marketing tactics with a complementary advertising campaign. Word of mouth is influenced by media as well as by champions you know by name. In your advertising campaign, use testimonials from experts, from celebrities or from satisfied clients. Focus on benefits and the unique selling advantage of your new service. Make the advertising action-oriented by encouraging the target clients to come to your office, call for information, place an order, write for more information or an appointment—some action that moves them forward toward the sale.

242. Follow up sales of the new product to evaluate customer satisfaction. Make refinements based on what you find. Most professional services are customized for each client. There is wide room for variability in service delivery. It pays to make sure that your service has met their expectations.

243. See each client as new. Treat the sale of each new product as if the client were the new element in the transaction—overwhelm the client with exceptional service, and then surprise him or her with something extra.

244. Develop an incentive program to get new product trials. New product introduction often requires some incentive for prospective clients to get past their indecision: coupons, special introductory offers, referral discounts, premium tie-ins, etc.

245. Make your product significant. New products are innovations only if they are perceived to be so by the consumer. Make sure that what you think is an innovation is also significant to your target buyers.

246. Be reviewed by an expert; win an award. These time-tested principles still work in getting magazine and newspaper editors and writers to pay attention. Send a free sample of your product to the editor along with a detailed letter stating its benefits and several possible "angles" that the editor can use in reviewing it. Do not ask for the product to be returned. Then make a follow-up telephone call to introduce yourself. If what you sell is a service, then send an introductory letter inviting the editor to your business to see the service demonstrated. Here are some of the ways the following industries have been successfully reviewed:

- Restaurant: Invite editor for complimentary dinner for two.
- Resort: Invitation for complimentary weekend for two.
- Book: Free copy sent to book review editor.
- Computer software: Complimentary copy sent to editor.
- Movie/theater: Free tickets for two.
- Packaged goods: Free product sample sent along with copies of competitor's products.

Don't forget trade journals and newsletters that often review new products. Organize a list of all relevant publications, including local and regional newspapers, magazines and newsletters. The same goes for official contests and awards programs.

*P*rofiles Of *S*uccess

Boston Beer Company
Boston, Massachusetts

Company Profile: Brewers of Samuel Adams beers.

Word-of-Mouth Tactics: During its first year in business, Boston Beer Company had no advertising budget. The high-energy sales efforts of the company's founder and president, Jim Koch, early publicity and news generated when the product was introduced led to word of mouth and sales. Although the company now has an advertising budget (which it uses primarily to educate consumers) and maintains relationships with the well-organized industry distribution system, word of mouth still plays an important role in retail establishments.

Within just a few months of introducing his grandfather's family-recipe beer, Jim Koch won a major beer award. A few months later, Boston Beer Company again made the news when it announced that it was exporting beer to Germany.

Early in the sales process, Koch realized the great influence bartenders and servers have in recommending products to customers. He then set out to develop relationships with these referral sources so that when a customer asked for a suggestion, servers recommended Samuel Adams beer. Through its professional sales force the company provides training programs, point-of-purchase merchandise such as shirts and hats, sponsorships and complimentary customized printed menu stands for any retailer carrying its products. In production now is a training video showing servers how to explain to customers the proper pairing of the most appropriate beer with various foods.

Direct-marketing tactics are used to maintain relationships with over 50,000 individuals who have shown an interest in the company either by writing a letter, taking the brewery tour or playing a key role in the distribution and retailing of the products. These individuals receive the company newsletter and any special information the company wants to pass on through its loyal supporters.

Results: Boston Beer Company does not track how much of its business results from word of mouth, as there are so many promotional tactics in the marketing plan. *(Used by permission from Boston Beer Company)*

Chapter 10

*C*oordinating Word of Mouth with Other Promotional Methods

"If it sounds too good to be true, it probably is."

— *Anonymous*

"I know I just wasted half of my advertising dollars, but I don't know which half."

— *American business lament*

*T*raditional marketing management is a blend of five elements:

1. Customers and their needs
2. The mix of products and services offered
3. Access to products and services
4. The cost to the customer
5. Promotional/communication methods

Word-of-mouth marketing is an all-weather tactic that is ideally suited for you when you are managing all these elements. It works during the good times of strong cash flow. It works during the hard times, too.

Customers and their needs.   Customers need information about products they buy and companies with which they do business. They need reassurance and assistance in decision making. Word-of-mouth marketing fulfills these needs directly and forcefully. It is the only form of advertising that is customized *by* consumers *for* consumers. Word of mouth is not the type of advertising you can buy; it must be earned day after day. In this chapter I recommend that you tap into this powerful form of communication and let it help you design your paid advertising.

129

The mix of products and services offered.   Marketing management involves creating the right mix of products and services to meet customers' needs. The root product or service that many professionals offer is competence and communication. Word-of-mouth marketing supports these two contributors to successful service by supplying the main topic of discussion when people talk. The core product that traditional product-based companies offer is the intangible meaning the product holds for the consumer. When word of mouth is part of the presale experience, consumers add to the product what they hear about it from others. In other words, word of mouth becomes part of the product itself in a discussion between a champion customer and a prospective customer.

Access to products and services.   Access to your services is crucial to meeting customers' needs. If customers can find you, get to see you quickly, feel socially accepted and feel that they can afford your services, they have access. Word-of-mouth marketing helps create access by informing a prospective customer of your existence and creating an expectation that they will find what they need in your business. Word of mouth tears down the barrier of mistrust, opening the way for someone to take a risk with your products. This is true for both final consumers and key players in the distribution networks through which your products or services flow.

The cost to the consumer.   Trust is an intangible part of the price consumers pay for the value you offer in your products. Word-of-mouth marketing makes it easier for them to give you their trust, because they have relied on the word of a person who is satisfied with your service. Like the continual quest for spiritual renewal, consumers in every culture continue to look for value. They want a better deal. They want to sense that what they get in value from you is greater or equal to the value they bring (in cash or trade) to you. So, if the tangible price of your product is low, this tends to generate more word of mouth.

Promotional/communication methods.   Communication to current customers, prospective customers and other referral sources (including champion customers) is important. What is lacking in the "sloganeering" of most advertising is more than made up for by the power and cost-effectiveness of word-of-mouth marketing. It never seems manipulative, and its appeal evokes a true humanitarian response. Because of its close ties to other marketing elements, and because it is an integrating force in all your marketing efforts, word-of-mouth marketing plans should guide your overall promotional efforts.

Advertising with Power

Consider how powerful word of mouth is from the perspective of the Gillette Company. When Gillette marketing executives introduced their new erasable ink pen, they first sent it to about 60,000 opinion leaders before releasing any advertising. A few weeks later, researchers surveyed the general population and found that up to 40 percent had heard of the product and 13 percent knew the brand name—all from word of mouth. With that kind of result, it is no wonder that the paid advertising had impact.

I have helped businesspeople who have tried almost every type of promotional method known. They have tried telephone marketing, direct marketing (through the mail or delivered directly to residences), radio advertising, public relations activities, newspapers and dozens of other ideas. Some of these promotional ideas work for some businesses, but that doesn't mean they will work for you in your community. Many of the traditional methods cost hundreds of dollars before delivering a return. Yet around every corner is someone who promises "results" if you will just buy this or that new program.

When advertising sales reps come around my office, my antennae go up to hear their promises. Politely I hear them out and then ask the key question: "What can you show me regarding your advertising program that will convince me that I will get new customers from the money I spend?" Then I encourage them to go back to their office and develop a program that will actually bring in new business. I tell them that when they have this completed, I will welcome them back to my office to discuss their findings. Not one has ever returned. I ask the question not to be difficult or to give them a hard time. It is a fair and fundamental question, and one that should be asked of any marketing tactic.

When they can think of no other reason for me to buy their advertising methods, I usually hear the claims of last-ditch sales efforts:

- "Advertising gets your name out there in the community." While this is true, it doesn't answer the question of what return I can expect from spending my money in the way they want.
- "Advertising shows support for _____." This sales tactic is often used by booster organizations that sell space in a printed event program. What they are really asking for is a donation—and it should be handled as a donation rather than an advertisement, which carries expectations for building new business.
- "Advertising builds community spirit." Rah rah! But that won't necessarily translate into new business. As a business owner, I want results from the money I spend on marketing.
- "All advertising is good, because it keeps your name in front of your customers and the public." This is a variation on the first reason and plays off the fear that if you don't buy space in their medium, your name will not be in front of people. In reality, it is your reputation that keeps your good name where it should be when it is needed.

Let me be clear: I have nothing against promotional methods that cost money. Launching a new product costs a lot of money in paid advertising, but paid advertising is vital to success of a new venture. I have nothing against advertising, advertising agencies or sales personnel who represent companies dependent on advertising revenue. They have a legitimate role in business. My point is that if you wish to engage in traditional promotional methods, do so after reviewing the following considerations.

Three Principles To Follow

First, don't advertise at the expense of your word-of-mouth marketing program, the champion customers who are working hard for you already. If you spend all your marketing resources on external advertising and public relations, you will have little left to devote to your champion customers, who are your best marketers. Why take your money out of the bank that gives you the best return and put it where you don't even know the interest rate? Why take the ammunition from the most powerful weapons of marketing in the heat of the battle? Start spending your marketing dollars on making champion customers: Serve them well, identify them, inform them, encourage them and thank them. Then, if you have marketing money left, buy a traditional promotional program that is consistent with the reputation you have built.

Second, don't engage in a promotional program that is inconsistent with the best word-of-mouth marketing program you can manage. I've seen promotional materials that looked like pizza advertising, but when I went to the company to meet the owners and look at the business, the atmosphere was nothing like that of a take-out pizza shop. They had wonderful new-customer orientation materials; they were consistent in watching out for small sources of irritation; and they treated their champion customers as if the world revolved around them. But their promotional materials portrayed a different image. The materials created confusion and weakened brand awareness.

Third, coordinate your word-of-mouth marketing so that its message gets to the right people at the right time. If you are convinced, for example, that direct marketing will get results for you, you may not wish to change your tactics. Using this method alone, however, without coordinating it with a word-of-mouth marketing program, is like using only four of the eight cylinders in the promotional engine. Don't ask "What other promotional methods will we use this year to bring in new customers?" Instead, ask "What additional promotional tactics should we employ that will help us increase word of mouth?"

I am convinced that as much as 50 percent of the advertising money spent by businesses is wasted because the buyers did not focus the advertising on building word-of-mouth marketing. Instead of informing, encouraging and rewarding the 20 to 40 percent of customers who are champions, they try to get a 1 or 2 percent response rate from prospective customers with a special offer through high-cost advertising. Which would you rather have coming through your door: prospective customers who are presold through word of mouth or customers who are wary, unsure and skeptical?

This sounds like I'm trying to pit word-of-mouth advertising against other tested approaches to promotion. I'm not. I'm simply making the point that word of mouth is the root and the integrating force in promotion. If you leave it out of your advertising budget, you are making a major mistake.

*A*ction *A*genda

247. *Use direct marketing.* If you use direct delivery marketing (that is, delivered by the U.S. Postal Service or a commercial delivery company) to communicate with specific neighborhoods or groups of consumers, first determine how comfortable you would feel sending the material only to your champion customers. Would you be embarrassed if your opinion leader customers received this material? Are you uncomfortable about making the same offer to your champions? If the answer to either question is yes, dump the program and start over. Your feelings on this issue are flags of reason that should not be ignored.

Direct marketing is the ultimate form of target marketing. You already have the names and addresses of hundreds of customers—the backbone of direct marketing work. If you start with a small list, such as your champions, you can control its elements to a great extent. Direct marketing is my favorite method for most businesses, because it confers benefits that no other paid promotional effort can match.

- You control exactly what the customer receives.
- You control exactly when the customer receives it.
- You control exactly who receives it.
- You can provide repeat exposures as often as you wish.
- You can develop a relationship through direct marketing, which you cannot do with other forms of promotion. (For every champion you don't capture through building a productive relationship, you lose the thousands of dollars those champions would have brought in.)
- You don't have limitations of space and format that other media command.
- Direct marketing can be made personal and confidential.

Direct marketing creates an environment that allows the recipient a way to respond, such as by coming to the store, calling your company, requesting more information or telling a friend to purchase a product.

248. *Test your direct marketing program on confirmed champions.* After you see their response, extend the campaign to prospective customers next.

249*. Send a series of personal letters to the top 50 confirmed champions.* Even if it costs something to communicate regularly with your champions, you will be rewarded with referrals many times. The following are some suggested topics:

- An award-winning design company just redecorated (or remodeled) our offices. You are invited for a personal tour.
- The owner of the company had an article published in the business newspaper. Enclosed is a summary, with our compliments.
- The owner recently attended a continuing education seminar on the topic of _____. He has written a summary of the material presented. We want to share this with you at no charge.
- We now have a new service available, because we just purchased or leased special equipment or hired a new staff person.
- We now have access to a new product: _____. If you, a family member or a friend have been thinking of making this type of purchase, you may come to our office to see it.
- The owner will be speaking at lunch on Wednesday of next week for the Leisure Manor retirement community. He has made special arrangements for you to attend.
- Please accept my sincere appreciation for sending such a thoughtful thank-you note. We have a notebook of these kinds of letters we like to share with new customers. May we have the honor of including your letter in the book?
- Congratulations on your retirement! I know this is a big change for you, and I want to hear more about your plans for the future.
- Recently the *Regional Business Journal* published an article on _____, and I wanted you to know about it. I am enclosing a short summary of the article with this letter. If you want more information on this topic, just call and ask to speak with _____.
- The office staff is planning a special week to honor our women customers. We invite you to attend our special open house next Wednesday from 4:00 to 7:30 PM. _____ will give a special presentation, and we will show a short video on how our products are manufactured.

250*. Boost the effectiveness of your direct marketing letters.* Personal direct marketing letters can be either long or short, depending on the subject covered and what you want to accomplish. Long letters will be read just as much as short ones if you keep customers' interest, so don't be afraid of long letters. Track the results of your direct marketing work. Some letters are just for maintaining a good relationship with customers; others are meant to get someone to take an action. These action-oriented letters require you to count the customers who call or come to your business. Tracking can also mean measuring the dollars you spend on direct marketing compared with what you collect from those who respond.

251. *Increase your champions' involvement.* Encourage them to recruit new customers to come to your company. Ask them for the names of people to whom you can send the information, making sure they understand that there is no obligation to become an active customer. This is a good chance for their friends to come in and meet you. If you continue to get positive feedback from your champions, ask them to take information about the offer to the community groups to which they belong. Supply them with small half-page fliers to pass out at meetings. It is acceptable to inform them that you will be spending only a minimal amount on promotion and would like them to help by communicating with people they know. The most important principle here is not to send out a mass mailing or mass delivery for the special program until you have worked your word-of-mouth network.

252. *Mine for gold in the gold mine.* Before you spend a few thousand dollars on promotion to unknown neighborhoods to get new customers, hire someone on a project basis to process a series of personal letters from you to each significant customer who honors you with a referral, customers who go through major life events and each new customer. These are just a few ideas. You will be able to think of many more. After you have developed your direct mail program to champions, you can expand it to include the neighborhoods where your customers live. Tell your customers what you are doing so that they can tell their neighbors about it and answer any questions the neighbors may have.

The letters will include reinforcement of the technical advice you gave them, statements of confidence that their quality of life will be improved and restatements of the benefits of your products. Offer to let them call you anytime they have a question. Communicate your appreciation for their trust in you and contribution to your reputation. Keep the letters short and personal. If you must use form letters, make sure you read each one you sign to check that they are appropriate for each customer's situation. Don't risk being embarrassed by sending a sympathy letter to a customer who is recovering from surgery. Keep a file of all the letters you send, and make notes on the ones that seem to generate the most enthusiasm or the most referrals. When a customer sends a written note in response to your letter, acknowledge that note the next time you see the customer.

253. *Critique your exterior signs.* Ask your champion customers for their evaluation of the sign on the exterior of your building. Would new customers have difficulty finding the building? Could they spot the sign quickly, or would they have to hunt for it? What exterior landmark is the best reference point for new customers? Would they have a difficult time finding your office in the building? Is the sign easy to read from the car? Is it easy for a new customer to find parking quickly? What would they change to make it easier for other customers to find you? All the information you glean here will be invaluable in helping you get new business: It helps you see reality from your customer's perspective. If you identify problems with your exterior sign, change it to meet the needs of your customers. You can get to your office with your eyes closed, but customers who have never been to the office or who come only once a year see it differently.

254. *Update your Yellow Pages advertising.* Expenditure for Yellow Pages advertising is on the increase among some industries as customers do more shopping from the convenience of their homes. Graphic artists can develop an attractive advertisement for your Yellow Pages listing. Your need to purchase display advertising depends on the type of community you are in. Smaller communities may not require more expensive display advertisements. It also depends on your industry and your specialty. If you find out through a survey of your clientele that a good proportion come to your business because of your Yellow Pages listing, don't dump your advertising thinking that word of mouth will make up for what is already routine for customers. When you design a Yellow Pages advertisement, make sure it is consistent with your reputation. Do not make glowing promises in the ad; this only sets up new customers for potential disappointment

later. Instead, communicate the facts and benefits clearly and suc-
cinctly. Remember that most new customers will depend on the word
of at least one other person even if they also see your advertisement.

255. *Track the results of your work qualitatively.*   Listen
to what others are saying about your company. Survey your customers. Conduct a focus group.

256. *Piggyback on the trends.*   Listen to what others are
talking about and get into the action. Write letters to prominent people
and display your letters and their responses in your business. Sponsor
a town hall meeting for opinion leaders to discuss the latest issues.

257. *Don't advertise your reputation for quality if the
reality is just the opposite.*   Some companies use mass media to try
to persuade consumers that they have high-quality products. They
boast and bluster about their excellence. This creates a problem if the
reality does not match the hype. If you have an image problem, now is
not the time to promote your image in your paid advertising. Your first
task is to get to the root of the image problem and correct it. Your paid
advertising should keep a low profile until the quality is improved to a
level acceptable to consumers. To promote your quality before that
happens will merely bring in new customers with high expectations.
These new customers will go away and tell others about the negative
experience they had. The rule of thumb is: Do your internal marketing
first and your external marketing second.

258. *List all your promotional methods.*   Next to each
method, list the amount of money you spent and the volume of known
business that resulted. Calculate the revenue per dollar spent for each
method. Check for yourself how word of mouth stacks up.

259. *Use product registration cards to track consumers.*   This is a widely accepted method of capturing names for
direct marketing. The information gathered on these cards should be
entered into a computer database for later use. Later you can send an
offer to those on your list and cull out the opinion leaders, marketing
mavens or product enthusiasts (based on the specific offer you make).

Those who respond should be flagged in the computer file as likely opinion leaders, marketing mavens, etc.

260. *Develop a lead card system.* A popular fitness center in the Los Angeles area uses this as its best method of getting word-of-mouth referrals. They printed up classy-looking point-of-purchase displays (complete with tear-off lead cards and a slotted receiving box) and personally distributed them to other retailers patronized by their target market. A sales representative of the fitness center visits the retailers weekly to pick up the lead cards. The weekly trips also give the sales rep the chance to talk with the retailers and give them new information to pass along to customers. Add an incentive for the retailer for higher levels of qualified leads generated (if appropriate) and you will have a dynamite system for word of mouth. Your incentive may be something simple and inexpensive, like dinner for two. Or it may be more exotic, depending on the revenue you make. If you use an incentive system, make sure your rewards are for qualified leads and not merely the number of cards turned in.

261. *Use the print medium.* It has been shown to be the best overall medium for reaching opinion leaders. First, they are hungry for the detailed information that only print can deliver. Second, you can target them better with print than with an electronic medium. Third, editorial comments about your product in the print medium are more valuable to opinion leaders than paid advertising.

262. *Remember that social pressure is a stronger influence on people than mass media.* Some advertisers question the importance of opinion leaders because they assert that everyone is, or will be, interested in the products they advertise. Don't be fooled by these so-called experts.

263. *Stimulate word of mouth through advertising.* You can accomplish this by doing the following:

- Target your mass media messages to opinion leaders (when you cannot contact them directly). In other words, advertise in print and electronic media that they use for gathering information.

- Suggest in your advertising that opinion seekers "ask their friends" or "ask a professional" about your product. You know that their friends will turn out to be opinion leaders.
- Pretest promotional messages with opinion leaders. This will stimulate word of mouth.
- Create advertisements with conversational value. True stories, dramatic demonstrations (if they are true and credible) and human interest stories are examples. If you use a demonstration that is so dramatic that very few will believe its validity, ask an independent testing company to verify your claim. Above all, avoid misleading the public by rigging the demonstration. As one of the leading automobile manufacturers learned a few years ago, misleading the public can backfire and cause negative word of mouth.
- Use headlines and slogans that are easily repeatable by consumers. Use consumer language. Give the types of information that opinion leaders are likely to be asked for by opinion seekers.
- Give your advertising entertainment value. Parodies on common human problems and caricatures of real-life situations that show humor are examples. If you use this approach, be careful to avoid sensitive issues, such as race, gender and religion.
- Use teaser campaigns that don't tell the whole story immediately. With these, roll out part of your advertising message one week at a time until after two or three weeks the whole message is given.
- Monitor to see if communication channels actually transmit the positive messages you intend. If there is negative information being transmitted, make changes immediately and communicate these to opinion leaders.
- Use paid advertising to report how much of your new business comes in because of word of mouth. If you can only estimate the proportion of business coming from referrals, do not mislead the public by being specific in your claims. If you faithfully gather statistics on the proportion of new customers coming in by word of mouth, show your statistics to prospective customers.
- Display copies of your advertising and publicity in your facility for prospective customers to view.

264. *Simulate word of mouth in your advertising.* Simulating word of mouth is one of the oldest themes used in paid advertising. This can be accomplished through the following:

- Advertising that depicts one person telling another about a product's benefits and the two of them then discussing the product's value. Try to use visual and audio cues to tell the target audience that the people in the advertisement are "just like them."
- Testimonials of a recent purchaser of the product. These will keep your message current. Show (or tell) dates and places to give the message extra validity.
- Testimonials by prominent people (experts or celebrities). Endorsers must be selected carefully so they will be seen as a valid information source.
- Emphasis on the kinds of people who buy the product. Use the leverage of the existing positive images of current users. This can be accomplished through visual images, descriptions given by the narrator and conversations between the actors.

265. Monitor to determine what people are saying about your product. After you start your paid advertising, do the following:

- Listen to customers to pick up the positive talk about your product. Then emphasize this positive talk (the actual words and phrases that consumers use in discussing your product with others) in future advertising. This monitoring will help you identify the strongest themes that will generate positive word of mouth.
- Combat negative information with more information or with positive information. If needed, make product refinements.

266. Complement media efforts with educational efforts. Educate opinion leaders and seekers on how to use the product as well as the benefits of owning it. Seminars should be designed to encourage opinion leaders to share their experience with others.

267. To manage a paid advertising program, concentrate on integration and execution. Integrate your paid advertising with the other elements of the marketing mix. Integration occurs when the themes and messages, the timing and the media are all consistent with the target audience. Integration also occurs when these elements are consistent with your pricing, your product and your distribution system. Then carefully execute the details of timing and intensity of the advertisements you buy.

***268**. Use your store windows, product fliers, promotional events, invoices and other envelope "stuffers" to build word of mouth.* When you identify the one or two major themes that constitute your company image in the community, incorporate them into all other promotional efforts, including direct sales. Before you develop a new printed communication tool, ask yourself or your marketing staff "How can this new tool help support our positive word-of-mouth marketing program?" Stay with the question till you get past the trite, safe answers.

***269**. Carefully select promotional events that boost word of mouth.* Promotional events, if conducted in a manner consistent with your company's image, can increase word of mouth. Examples of promotional events include the following:

- Seasonal and holiday sales events
- Contests, sweepstakes, awards and gift drawings
- In-store displays, exhibits and live entertainment
- Appearances by celebrities and sports figures
- Community involvement through sponsorships
- Frequent-buyer programs

Manufacturing companies, distributors, retailers, the travel industry and even the entertainment industry all use promotional events successfully. Special promotions generate more customer interest, stimulate word of mouth, and give the host company a means to gather detailed information on champion customers that can be used in database marketing and in improving the quality of service to champions. However, professional services have found that consumers do not respond well to promotions. For example, there is something not quite right about a real estate broker or an attorney offering a Valentine's Day special price on professional services. When deciding what type of promotional event to use, ask yourself the following questions:

- Will the event attract new customers?
- Will the event attract the right type of customer?
- Will the event support my image in the community?
- Will it cause service problems for customers?
- Will it be profitable?

270. Explore the use of new technology to boost word of mouth.   Advertising messages have traditionally spoken to consumers through newspapers, radio, television, magazines and direct mail. Opinion leaders seek information in a variety of venues, including the new computer-based technologies. Computer on-line information services, interactive computer presentations on diskette and the newly emerging field of interactive television are examples to consider.

An organization I served that wanted to attract other businesses as clients decided to use an interactive computer presentation on diskette. The diskette I created contained full-color graphics, huge amounts of information on the company and complete user control through the use of decision buttons. Although the diskette contained a lot of information, the consumer had control over how much information to view and in what order. We mailed the diskette to a selected group of potential business clients. This unusual promotional tactic resulted in the diskette being passed around from computer to computer inside the offices of a potential client. In more than one case, groups of decision makers in a potential client's company gathered around a computer to participate in the presentation together. This is much more powerful word of mouth than what most printed direct mail material can generate on its own.

271. Use coupons to increase word of mouth.   Create coupons that champions can give to their friends and neighbors. The coupon should include a space for the date, the opinion leader's name, address, phone number, etc., and space for the referral customer's information. Coupons should state that they are not valid unless this information is complete. If you already know who your champions are, give them the coupons. If you want to identify the champions, give every customer a coupon. Coupons that are returned will have the information you need on who the champions are. One housing development company sent out coupons worth $500 in cash for anyone who made a referral that resulted in the purchase of one of their new homes. The 8" x 10" coupons, which looked like official certificates, were sent with a cover letter to people who already lived in the area where the homes were constructed. The program was designed to attract potential customers who had never visited the model homes.

Another company printed up smaller coupons that resulted in a champion customer receiving a gift certificate worth $15 when a customer he or she referred made a purchase. This company tracked the results carefully and attributed 5 percent of the new business it received from the coupon referrals. This is a decent response for any direct mail program. What made it even more important is that the average value of purchases made by new customers using coupons was over $2,000.

272. Make a plan and follow it. The following is a sample six-month promotion plan that you can adapt to your company.

Sample Six-Month Integrated Campaign

Month 1—Getting Organized

1. Set objectives for the year. Make them specific, measurable, challenging and achievable.
2. Begin gathering names and addresses of opinion leaders, marketing mavens and product enthusiasts. Put this information in a computer database for later reference.
3. Begin talking with these champion customers regarding the image your company projects to the target audience. Conduct a focus group or a written opinion survey.
4. Establish a simple procedure for identifying, encouraging and rewarding champions who bring you other business. Start tracking results immediately.
5. Evaluate the paid advertising you did last year to determine which advertisements were targeted toward opinion leaders. Evaluate the contributions of your paid advertising toward developing a stronger brand awareness.
6. Determine which advertising resulted in the biggest payoff. Make a chart depicting the proportion of revenue (or profit) generated by each advertising method. This is your benchmark.

Month 2—Developing Your Advertising Campaign

1. Refine your program for identifying, encouraging and rewarding champions. Make improvements and continue tracking results.

2. Based on the research you conducted, develop a theme for your advertising that will:

   - support and strengthen the brand image.
   - be consistent with the positive word of mouth of champions.
   - clearly communicate what you want champions to be saying to opinion seekers.
   - clearly communicate the benefits of your product.
   - elicit a consumer action in response to the campaign.

   If you will emphasize testimonials, make sure you have actual testimonials on file. Get written permission from customers to use their words.

3. Determine which media will best target champion customers. Direct mail? A trade newsletter? The local newspaper? Remember to include marketing mavens and product enthusiasts. Gather information on the cost of advertising in your best choices. Select the frequency and the reach of your advertising. Try to target your audience as carefully as possible to minimize waste. If you decide that you should advertise directly to opinion seekers rather than opinion leaders, make sure your theme is consistent with the medium you select.

4. Based on your research, develop a budget you can live with. Evaluate what you spent in the past. Look for ways to save on the cost of paid advertising. Spread the costs of your promotion program over the entire year so that your cash flow will not be at risk.

5. Develop a public relations kit that communicates the theme and essential message of your advertising program. Hold this kit in readiness for the right time to send it out so that it is complementary to your advertising.

Month 3—Ready for Implementation

1. Continue to refine your word-of-mouth promotion efforts targeted to your current opinion leaders. Conduct more staff training. Refine the quality of your products and services.

2. Create the messages conveyed in your advertising. Write the copy and develop the graphic image. Make sure these two elements are consistent with your brand image.

3. Carefully time the release of your advertising and public relations kits. Publicity may be released simultaneously to or just preceding the first advertising messages.
4. Develop all point-of-purchase displays that will be used along with the paid advertising.
5. Train your staff on the details of your advertising campaign. Your employees should know all the details and policies of special offers, discounts and returns, as well as their responsibilities when new customers come as a result of the advertising. Rehearse their roles until you know they can perform them flawlessly.
6. Print all certificates, coupons and invitations if you use these materials.

Month 4—Manage an Integrated Effort

1. Set up a point-of-purchase display emphasizing the elements in your advertising campaign. All current customers should be informed first. Begin telling customers to watch for more information in the selected media.
2. Send information to your champion customers first through direct mail. Do this *before* public relations kits are sent to the media.
3. Target neighborhood newspapers or electronic media in areas where opinion leaders live. Send your press kits and purchase advertising to be released at the time of or just after press releases are published.
4. Send direct mail information to other opinion leaders, marketing mavens and product enthusiasts who are not customers but who can influence customers.
5. Continue to gather names of opinion leaders who buy from you.

Month 5—Emphasize Responsiveness to New Customers

1. Monitor the performance of all employees as it relates to your advertising program. Refine their work through additional training. Make sure your tracking system is working.
2. Emphasize the point-of-purchase display to all new customers.
3. Begin looking for more opinion leaders among new customers.
4. Conduct a telephone campaign with known opinion leaders telling them about your campaign and soliciting their support.

Month 6—Continue To Monitor Results

1. Carefully track the source of every new customer to determine who told them about your program or, if they saw your products in paid advertising, where they saw (or heard) your messages. Add new champion names to your computer database.

2. Monitor the attitudes of opinion leaders regarding your advertising. Determine whether your theme and message are consistent with the best word of mouth already happening. You can conduct another focus group or perform a telephone poll. Add to this the information you gather from customers who come in to buy from you.

3. Send another direct mail piece to opinion leaders thanking them for their hard work.

4. Before you send out your next installment of paid advertising to print and electronic media, evaluate the results of your work and make adjustments as necessary.

*P*rofiles Of *S*uccess

Callaway Golf Company
Carlsbad, California

Company Profile: Manufacturer and distributor of high-performance golf clubs.

Word-of-Mouth Tactics: Callaway Golf Company is an example of how to blend promotion tactics that build word of mouth with paid advertising. Bruce Parker, director of sales, says that the company spends heavily on print and television advertising messages that feature both golf and nongolf celebrities as spokespersons.

"The most effective advertising we have," says Parker, "is word of mouth." He comments that although the foundation for positive word of mouth is a quality product and excellent service after the sale, it is not the product that sells itself. Rather, it is the satisfied customer who sells the product to other customers after he or she has experienced it. Thus, most of the word-of-mouth tactics are built around the concept of letting the new customer see and feel firsthand the superior performance of the product.

The Callaway sales staff play a key role in building word of mouth when they visit golf pro shops and conduct live demonstrations of the Callaway clubs, including the famous "Big Bertha" drivers. At these demonstrations, golfing consumers actually get to "test drive" the clubs on the driving range. "When golfers see how easy the clubs are to use in their own hands and how much better they can perform with the clubs, they're sold—and they begin talking about it to others," says Parker.

Company sales staff also provide in-depth information to retail store managers and their sales staff in the form of one-hour product seminars offered right in their stores. The more information retail sales clerks have about the Callaway products, the more effective they are in referring customers to them.

Customer service at Callaway Golf Company is known in the industry as being superior. "We have never turned down a warranty claim," says Parker. "If a customer breaks a club and calls us about it, we nearly always send the golfer a brand new club by overnight express."

Callaway Golf also gives tours of its manufacturing facilities twice every business day for golf enthusiasts traveling through the area who are interested in seeing how the company builds quality into the product.

Results: Parker estimates that about 50 percent of sales to new customers results from word of mouth and 50 percent from print and television advertising. *(Used by permission from Callaway Golf Company)*

Chapter 11

*A*ssessing the Cost
of Word of Mouth

*"*Talk is cheap.*"*

— American proverb

I've already mentioned that word-of-mouth marketing is not free. It costs you something to offer excellent service. Higher-quality products may cost more to produce than ones of lower-quality if materials or production processes are more expensive. However, there are many quality experts who assert that, for similar products, those of higher quality cost less to produce in the long run than those of lower quality.

Typically, the more services you provide, the more it will cost you in employee wages and benefits or new technology. Discount retailers have learned this principle many times over. A discount retailer enters the market boasting low prices to attract the price-sensitive customers. Quantity buying and self-service are emphasized. As other discount retailers set up shop near by, the basis of competition shifts from price alone to price *and* service. More employees are hired. Upgraded merchandising tactics inform consumers about the products, their prices and quality. This added service promotes positive word of mouth.

Therefore, the issue examined in this chapter is not whether there are costs associated with added service. The issues here are

- whether it costs more not to have a word-of-mouth marketing program than to have one, and
- whether the other elements of word-of-mouth promotion cost you more than other forms of promotion.

Three Important Principles

There are three basic points I want to emphasize:

1. Positive word of mouth will cost less cash and will bring a larger return on investment than most other promotional methods.
2. Negative word of mouth will cause a loss of potential revenue and probably some cash. It can easily cancel out positive word-of-mouth marketing.
3. Without a word-of-mouth marketing program that addresses both the negative and positive dynamics, your other promotional efforts will probably cost more.

Here's what I mean. First, positive word-of-mouth marketing costs less than other forms of promotion. Asking for a referral costs nothing, so when a satisfied customer recommends you to someone else, you are getting something for nothing. You can't beat that. Even if you decide to spend a little cash to show appreciation, you can spend it *after* the referral has brought you revenue, so you're still not out anything. Where else can you pay for your marketing efforts after you have benefited from those efforts? Every other form of promotion requires that you risk money without a guaranteed return. The only cost involved with word-of-mouth marketing is your expense for the labor that is expended in the course of providing excellent service.

Second, positive word-of-mouth marketing traditionally produces a better return on your promotional investment. If you spent $5,000 on a year-long advertising campaign, what financial return would you get? I recently did some research in a southern California city, and below is a summary of what I found as I compared several promotional tactics. (I realize that not all geographic areas are the same in terms of marketing costs.)

A Comparison of Promotion Methods

Yellow Pages.   For $5,000 you could get about a one-fifth-page, one-color ad, plus two column listings. The response to the ad will depend on how much consumer demand exists for the product. You could get one or two new clients a month or ten each day. Track the results carefully. Some businesses get 10 or even 15 percent of all their new clients from Yellow Pages advertising.

One small-business owner did a test of his Yellow Pages advertising to determine its effectiveness. He purchased a separate phone line with a previously unpublished number. He advertised the new number in one Yellow Pages book only. As a result, he averaged about 30 calls a month on the new phone line. This didn't translate into 30 new clients each month, however. Some of the calls were from existing clients who had to look up his number in the Yellow Pages. Some of the callers had the wrong number. A few were interested in his services and became new clients.

For some retail businesses, Yellow Pages are the lifeline to new customers. If you are not in the book, you don't stay in business. But even if your business has traditionally depended on the Yellow Pages for new customers, don't count out the power of word of mouth. With a strong word-of-mouth marketing program, your Yellow Pages advertising will be even more effective.

Newspaper.   For $5,000 you can get one quarter-page ad in a local daily paper six times a year or the same size ad in a weekly paper a dozen or so times a year. To be effective, most newspaper advertisements must include a special offer or something that will attract customers. I've seen businesses waste thousands of dollars on newspaper advertising when following the well-meaning counsel of a marketing consultant.

There is nothing wrong with newspaper advertising. Businesses that use coupons or that attract customers who depend on the newspaper for marketplace information must continue to use this medium. Don't dump your ad campaign because you get excited about word of mouth, but recognize that word of mouth will probably cost you less per client than paid advertising. Also recognize that there may be an opportunity to refine your paid advertising programs to tap into the power of word of mouth.

Company Brochures.   The company brochure is the most misunderstood marketing tool. Many professionals believe they need one but don't know how to use it. A company brochure can be helpful in a word-of-mouth marketing program, sit on a shelf or be used haphazardly. It represents a large marketing expenditure. Including design, copywriting, photos and printing, you can easily spend over $5,000 to get 3,500 or 4,000 copies. For now, just consider those costs compared with the low-cost word-of-mouth marketing tactics.

The results generated by a brochure will depend on how you use it. They will be difficult to track unless the brochure promotes a special offer and is distributed to new people. Word-of-mouth marketing can function without a brochure, because the strength of the program lies not in the printed page but in the power of a personal recommendation offered by a satisfied client.

Multimedia Computer Presentations.   This is one of the fastest-growing promotional methods for businesses that have a complicated product or service, or one that is difficult to describe to the customer. Multimedia computer demonstrations help the prospective customer to see what he or she will be buying. The sharing of computer disks among users is a growing trend that has emerged as the newest form of word-of-mouth marketing.

The cost of production can range from $1,500 to $10,000, depending on how sophisticated the demonstration is. Although an impersonal communication method, interactive multimedia computer demonstrations are a powerful form of promotion. Interaction is the key to consumer involvement. This qualifies as word-of-mouth marketing, because the new customer has a chance to ask specific questions of a company representative.

Tied in with other word-of-mouth tactics, this is a dynamic advertising method. If you use computer demonstrations, make it clear that your disk can be freely copied and given to anyone. Give your most important clients copies to give to other people.

Videos.   It is difficult to find a producer who will create a professional-quality video for less than about $1,000 per minute of completed videotape. Many production companies charge between $5,000 and $10,000 just to get started. As with multimedia computer presentations, videotapes have complementary value for word-of-mouth marketing programs, because people loan tapes to each other. If you do use videos, make it clear to clients that tapes can be freely copied and shared with others.

Direct Delivery. For $5,000 you can have professionally printed "door hangers" delivered five times a year to 8,000 households or businesses. I've tried this type of promotional tactic. It works well for businesses that have customers who rely on coupons as cues for purchasing. Direct delivery has an advantage over direct mail in that it does not compete with other messages for the potential client's attention. I am a firm believer in direct marketing, but used in a one-time burst into a neighborhood, it doesn't compare with a long-term, consistently applied internal-marketing program that develops word of mouth. Used on a consistent basis and combined with other word-of-mouth tactics, direct delivery can be a powerhouse promotion for you. Word-of-mouth results may be slower to develop than results generated by direct marketing, but the staying power of word of mouth is infinitely stronger and much less expensive.

Word of Mouth. Take your top clients and spend between $25 and $50 on them each year to acknowledge their referrals, and give them superior service. Show them how much you appreciate their referrals and you will get more. Remember, this expense is incurred *after* they do the work for you. Overwhelm the new clients they bring in with excellent service. One advantage to this type of promotion is that often you don't need to spend the $50 on each champion client to get them to generate referrals.

Return on Investment

Throughout this book, I have mentioned return on investment as if it were a magical litmus test for marketing. I've also made the claim that word-of-mouth marketing will produce high rates of return on a promotional investment. Even if this is true for you, what does it mean? Some marketing consultants will tell you that a ten to one return on investment gives you $10 of gross revenue for every dollar you spend on promotion. The following is an example of how to calculate the return on investment.

Suppose you spent $1,000 on a promotional program to build business volume. With a tracking system in place, you can confirm that you bring in 50 new customers, each buying an average of $100 worth of products. Your return on investment (ROI) is five to one. An ROI of five to one would be dramatic results from any type of promotion.

This is a rather crude way of reckoning ROI, but some find it useful. I prefer to include in the formula a factor for what it costs you to sell the product to the 50 new customers (in other words, basing ROI on an estimated *net* pretax revenue rather than on gross revenue).

With my personal addition to the formula, the return drops to a lower level. Using the same example and subtracting 50 percent for the expenses involved in performing the service, your return on investment will be 2.5 to 1. Whether you choose my method or the simpler version, stick to it to compare one promotional method with another. Be sure to track your results.

The Costs of Negative Word of Mouth

This is where you probably expect me to bring down the hammer on negative word of mouth. I won't disappoint you, because it helps make the point about how important a positive word-of-mouth marketing program is.

Five sources of cost result from negative word of mouth:

1. Lost revenue occurs when unhappy clients decide to go to another company. You could argue that this doesn't really take cash out of your pocket, and I would grant you this much. However, if these clients had remained satisfied with your organization, all things being equal, they would have returned to you and you would have made more money. The insidious thing about this type of lost revenue is that it happens very slowly.

2. You may have to increase your advertising expenditures to offset the effects of negative word of mouth. If your advertising budget is climbing, look at the elements of your word-of-mouth marketing. You will probably be able to reduce your paid advertising as negative word of mouth is reduced and as positive word of mouth begins to have an impact.

3. There are costs involved in replacing dissatisfied clients who take their business elsewhere. The rule of thumb is that it costs a business as much as five times more to capture a new consumer than it costs to keep a happy one. Replacement costs for dissatis-

fied clients can represent cash out of your pocket if you want to maintain the volume you had before losing the unhappy clients.

Replacement costs are most significant for products that are purchased infrequently, such as home appliances, episodic health care, automobiles, machinery and computers. In these cases, if you lose a customer, you may have lost him or her for up to 15 years. If their next two purchases are influenced by the negative experience they had with your product, the total loss potential per customer can be in the six-digit range.

Over a span of ten years, a customer may purchase automobiles three or four times. The net worth of this customer to automobile manufacturers is well over $100,000. To a computer manufacturer, the ten-year net worth of a customer represents over $10,000 for a personal computer and hundreds of thousands of dollars for mainframe units. A consulting firm that loses a renewable contract can quickly lose in one day the potential for making $50,000 to $100,000.

Brand switching alone accounts for a large portion of lost revenue to many companies. Consider these sobering numbers for a manufacturer that wholesales a product for $100. This manufacturer receives 100 complaints a year from one state. If this represents just 5 percent of all unhappy customers, the others who are unhappy but don't complain number approximately 1,900 for the year. If just 25 percent of the 1,900 unhappy customers simply switch brands, the manufacturer is losing 475 customers representing $47,500 in lost revenue.

Applying these assumptions across a much larger market, such as a country as large as the United States, the lost revenue from brand switching could cost a company more than $2 million. The distributors and retailers who carry this same product represent a combined loss of over $4 million.

4. The fourth source of cost is more difficult to calculate. If you have a problem with negative word of mouth, you are going to miss the opportunity to serve some clients who would have come to you if they had not heard horror stories. Counting actual numbers here is impossible.

5. Other sources of cost include the amount of staff time that it takes to solve problems and deal with unhappy clients, legal and

insurance expenses, and lower productivity. In some businesses these costs can be monitored.

The Cost of Positive Word of Mouth

Costs of managing positive word-of-mouth programs can be broken down into four categories:

1. Spending cash on identifying, encouraging and acknowledging your champion customers. A successful word-of-mouth marketing program does not require a large expense for these items.
2. Giving discounts (in the form of coupons or certificates) to champion customers when they refer others to you. This may not be cash out of the register, but it is cost because it represents a lower profit margin.
3. Reducing prices to generate customer conversation. If a company lowers its price dramatically, people talk about it (especially marketing mavens and product enthusiasts). This is one tactic to generate positive word of mouth. However, lowering your price will cost you in profit margin. If you can make up for the decrease in profit by selling a higher volume, the net result may be an increase.
4. Adding service costs. However, as in the example of the popular clothing marketer Liz Claiborne, added service sometimes *pays*. Liz Claiborne sales personnel are trained to groom their champion customers and tend to every detail of their clothing-purchase needs. They know every champion by name and keep careful records on the tastes of these powerful marketing resources, as well as those of their family and friends. People are willing to pay more for excellent service when they know it is genuine and consistent. Unfortunately, service is one of the first elements of a business to be cut when a financial crisis hits. Often this occurs because there is no clear perceived connection between service and profits at the top executive level.

Positive word of mouth pays in several ways. To begin with, marketing and sales costs per customer are lower. It costs you less to bring in a new customer who is already presold by one of your champions.

When your organization has a strong champion-cultivating program, positive word of mouth pays as the cost of maintaining their loyalty is reduced. You know a lot about their consumer needs and interests (information that is very expensive to get for people who are not customers). You spend little or nothing on checking their credit, because you have already done that. You already have champions in your database (it costs to add *new* names and related information to your database).

People who talk positively about a company tend to purchase more products from that company. This means that the annual net worth of one champion will be much higher than one new customer.

Finally, customers who come by word of mouth may be willing to pay more for your products and services because of your reputation.

Figures 11.1 and 11.2 summarize the costs of negative word of mouth and the value of positive word of mouth. The actual dollar amounts can be adjusted for your situation. Larger businesses will have a more complex revenue picture.

Not included in these figures are other costs involved with the results of negative word of mouth, such as legal fees, office inefficiency, waste and low productivity. When calculating the potential annual loss for your business, estimate the *annual* revenue from each customer, recognizing that customers may patronize your business more than once each year.

Your Word-of-Mouth Assets

Can you account for your word-of-mouth assets? An asset is usually defined as cash that you have now or a legal right to cash in the future. Is your reputation an asset? The financial experts may debate this, but consider the cash-generating power of champion customers.

First, all else being equal, champion customers can be expected to continue referring others to you over time if you maintain a positive relationship with them. The actual length of time they will support your company with recommendations depends upon your ability to fend off the actions of competitors, how well you can maintain quality and how well you can respond to changing consumer demands. While it is true that you have no legal right to the actions of satisfied champion customers, you can expect that they will support your company in the future (by positive talk) based on evidence of their past behavior. Goodwill has a certain momentum fueled by your continued attention to word-of-mouth marketing tactics.

Second, some businesses can count accurately how much revenue or profit is generated by word of mouth. Other businesses can estimate the word-of-mouth revenue. In the short term, you can learn to predict with amazing accuracy how much business will come in next week or next month because of word of mouth.

FIGURE 11.1 The Cost of Negative Word of Mouth

Revenue from Positive Word of Mouth	
None	$0
Lost Revenue	
Annual gross revenue	$400,000
Number of clients	2,000
Percentage of clients who leave	18.75%
(assume 25% are dissatisfied and 75% of these leave)	
Number of dissatisfied clients who leave	375
Average revenue per client per year	$ 250
Lost Revenue	$ 93,750
(375 x $250)	
Replacement Costs	
Marketing costs	$ 8,000
Average cost per client	$ 4
Marketing costs for 375 lost clients	$ 1,500
Multiplied by a factor of 5 for replacement	$ 7,500
(375 x $4 x 5)	
Summary	
Revenue from positive word of mouth	$ 0
Lost revenue	-$ 93,750
Replacement costs	-$ 7,500
Total Negative Results	($101,250)

Results over ten years = a loss of $1,012,500.

FIGURE 11.2　The Value of Positive Word of Mouth

Here are the results achieved by the company depicted in Figure 11.1 after it establishes a word-of-mouth marketing program. Through a more consistent customer service program, the losses experienced as a result of negative word of mouth are minimized, although not completely eliminated.

Revenue from Positive Word of Mouth

Number of referrals made by satisfied clients	2,400
(assume 30% recommend you to four others)	
Number of new clients gained	240
(assume 10% respond)	
New revenue from positive word of mouth	$ 60,000
(240 x $250)	

Lost Revenue

Annual gross revenue	$ 400,000
Number of clients	2,000
Percentage of dissatisfied clients who leave	2.5%
(assume 5% unhappy and 50% of these leave)	
Number of dissatisfied clients	50
Average revenue per client per year	$　250
Revenue lost through negative word of mouth	$　12,500
(50 x $150)	

Replacement Costs

Marketing costs	$　8,000
Marketing costs per client	$　4
Marketing costs for 50 lost clients	$　200
Multiplied by 5 for replacement	$　1,000
(50 x $4 x 5)	

Summary

Revenue from positive word of mouth	$　60,000
Lost revenue	-12,500
Replacement costs	-1,000
Total positive results	$　46,500

Results over ten years = an increase of $465,000, an annual gain of almost $146,000 compared with the costs shown in Figure 11.1.

Action Agenda

273. *Calculate how much word of mouth is worth to you.*
Fill in the form below to find out its value to your business.

1. _____ new customers purchase our products or services every month (or year).
2. _____ % of new customers purchase our products or services because of a recommendation from someone else (do not include sales personnel).
3. $_____ gross revenue is usually received from every new customer who remains loyal to our products or services for 10 years.
4. $_____ net revenue or profit is generated by each referral that results in a new customer.
5. _____ % of company profit is accounted for by word of mouth.
6. _____ % of customers in our company are confirmed champions who make recommendations on our behalf.
7. _____ is the number of new customers that each confirmed champion brings to us each year.

Some of the information requested in this form will have to be based on your best estimate. Large manufacturing firms will have more difficulty gathering this information than will retailers and service companies. If you find that you cannot fill in more than one or two blanks on this form, begin a survey of word of mouth referrals. Get to know how much financial leverage you have with your company's word-of-mouth market.

274. *Calculate the impact of negative word of mouth.* Fill in the form below using figures from your business. For some companies, some of the information requested below will have to be estimated rather than calculated.

1. Divide your annual profit by the total number of customers you serve each year: _____ dollars per customer per year
2. Estimate the number of customers who leave your business due to factors that you can control: _____ customers
3. Multiply your answer in 2 by the answer in 1: $ _____ dollars

4. Calculate or estimate the total annual cost of promotion: $_____

5. Multiply your answer for 2 times your answer for 4 times five: $_____

6. Add your answer for 3 to your answer for 5: $ _____

This is an estimate of what negative word of mouth costs you.

*P*rofiles Of *S*uccess

James Armel, Prudential California Realty
Rancho Cucamonga, California

Company Profile: Residential and commercial real estate sales

Word-of-Mouth Tactics: "The two key lessons I have learned the last ten years as a real estate professional," says James Armel, "are providing quality service and exceeding the expectations of clients— underpromise and overdeliver." This is the reason most of his business comes through word of mouth.

Armel uses a variety of approaches, all of which contribute to building referrals. These include the following:

1. He is consistently involved with his community through school programs, children's sporting events and service organizations. He calls it "marketing by hanging around."

2. He receives many testimonial letters but carefully selects which ones he uses to attract new customers. "I choose recommendations from stable, successful professionals to communicate with a similar target client," he says.

3. He blends word-of-mouth testimonials with his direct mail campaigns.

4. He identifies each referral by name, then customizes an acknowledgment for that person. Sometimes he simply sends a thank-you letter. Other times he may send a modest gift or gift certificate. Each situation and each person is different, requiring an approach that is appropriate for the setting. For clients who have been

especially supportive, he commemorates the anniversary of the sale (or purchase) of their home by sending them a holiday gift or offering a catered housewarming to which their family and close friends are invited.

5. He blends the use of stories with a telemarketing and direct mail campaign to communicate to potential clients that they will achieve success through a relationship with him.

6. He pursues the trust of new clients in a manner that communicates how he will serve them if they decide to sign up with him. This is a subtle method to help them test drive a relationship before they sign a contract.

7. He maintains a positive relationship with former clients for as long as they live in the region.

One day Armel received a call from an executive of a manufacturing firm who, along with many others, was being transferred to another city. Due to the quality service Armel provided this executive, 12 other company managers retained him to handle the sale of their property.

Results: Almost all of Armel's business comes from referrals. This saves him thousands of dollars annually in advertising expenses. *(Used by permission from James Armel, Prudential California Realty)*

Chapter 12

*U*sing the Power of Emotions To Build Your Business

*"*When dealing with people, remember you are not dealing with creatures of logic but with creatures of emotion.*"*

— Dale Carnegie

*"*He who can suppress a moment's anger may prevent a day of sorrow.*"*

— Ancient proverb

*W*hen you hear by the grapevine that a customer is talking up your business to others, rest assured it is not just the facts that are being spread. And it is not just the facts that are changing the prospective client's attitudes about you. Facts without meaning and feelings will die on the grapevine before they get a chance to work for you. People want to know that what your champion client experienced is significant—that it has meaning. They want reassurance that they will feel as good about it as your champion did.

Your positive reputation is carried on the wings of emotions like surprise, gratitude, acceptance, expectancy, happiness, relief and excitement. People talk because they feel.

Likewise, if a negative reputation is spread about you, it is carried on the flames of anger, disappointment, sadness, disgust, hurt, frustration, fear and confusion.

Emotions are the signals of what satisfaction or dissatisfaction means to clients. The feelings clients experience occur during a transaction, while they use your product, because they own your product or when they bring a complaint to you. All of these situations are interesting to prospective clients who talk with opinion leaders. People want to know *why* a buyer is satisfied with your product or with your company. They want to know the *meaning* of any dissatisfaction your client may have had. The meaning behind the feelings helps them predict whether purchasing from you will be a satisfying experience or not. At its most rudimentary level, this *meaning* is at the core of what is transferred to prospective customers during word of mouth.

When celebrities represent a product, they are transferring the intended meaning of a product's use or possession to prospective customers. This is one reason celebrities are used in promotional tactics: The power of their position is similar to the power of word of mouth from ordinary people. The celebrity brings not only the meaning of the product, its possession or its use to consumers, but also the meaning of who he or she is. If a celebrity represents prestige and status to consumers, these qualities are transferred to the product he or she represents. If they represent sensual pleasure, this meaning is transferred through the product they endorse. And if there is congruence between this quality and the product, the consumer begins to associate sensual pleasure with the product. In other words, celebrities are successful in endorsement when they create an association between consumers' feelings about the celebrity's highly visible world and the endorsed product.

You can give voice to the intended meaning of your products or services by tapping into a celebrity's power as long as there is a connection between the meaning the celebrity holds for your consumers and your product's meaning. On a small scale, every champion customer has the power of a celebrity when he or she talks to others on your behalf. At an emotional level, they transfer the core of what it means to buy, use or possess your products.

If you use an emotional sales appeal to a prospective client, you may or may not be successful. Most of the time it is better to use a reasoned approach rather than raw emotion. With many products and services, it is a risk for you to sell at the feeling level, as this will be manipulative. But your champion clients can get away with using direct emotional appeals all they want. They can tell how they feel about you all day long and prospective clients will soak it up, because it communicates to them at their core.

I've recommended that you give your champion clients plenty to talk about—plenty of details and facts about you and your company. Unless they have a positive emotional experience with your company, however, all the facts and details will mean little when it comes to spreading your good reputation. And if they are angry about something, all the logic and reasoning in your lifetime will not prevent them from spreading negative word of mouth about you. If you fail to deal with them at a feeling level, you lose. If you deal with them at a feeling level, provided there is substance to your work, you win. It's that simple.

The Power of Emotions in Business

Emotional response comes from personal experience—something that is almost impossible to give your clients through advertising. They do not emotionally respond to a brochure unless it reminds them of their own experience or the experience of someone they can empathize with. A newspaper advertisement is insufficient to generate emotion unless it features a real-life situation or a prominent celebrity testimonial. If you want clients to talk about you, give them a personal experience that generates an emotional response.

Business relationships are filled with your own emotions. If it weren't for the passion that the entrepreneur feels deep inside his or her soul, little would get done for profit and growth. Emotions can energize to action, and they also can immobilize to inaction. You may believe that you make business decisions on facts, logic and reason. This is only partially true, for most business decisions are also emotional decisions. Most business actions are emotional actions. And the more important the decision or action, the more intense the emotions surrounding the event.

When we evaluate business facts, we often get a gut feeling for the information and what it is telling us. We may be either correct or incorrect as we interpret business information. If we are incorrect, we may set ourselves up for business mistakes. Even if we are correct in our interpretation, we still have to deal with our own emotional response to it.

Life is a continuous experience and not segmented. Emotion is as much a part of marketing management as is the marketing mix of product, pricing, promotion and distribution. I am not suggesting that feelings prevent one from making rational business decisions, although that does happen. Instead, I am suggesting that our gut feelings about business information and what it means are based on logic and reason. Indeed, if we were not analyzing the data and making some kind of sense out of it, it would be meaningless, and we would feel nothing. Emotions are often the flags that signal what the information means to us.

Your Clients Have Emotions Too

Your clients also have emotions before, during and after their purchase of your product or service. The choice of one company over another may seem to be based on impulse. And sometimes what appears to us to be unfair bias may be, to the client, the most important factor in a purchase decision. Here are five ways that client bias creeps into the decision:

1. The first impressions the client has of you and your business
2. Your appearance and the appearance of your place of business
3. The history your client brings, including stereotypes, expectations, memories of other business relationships
4. Snap judgments about your products or services without consideration of all the evidence
5. Reliance on what appears to be irrelevant information

Don't discount the importance of certain things just because you disagree with whether clients should be affected by them.

Advertising experts have been attempting to tap into the power of emotions for years. They have found that positive feelings are aroused in clients when

- we satisfy the need to acquire, conserve, retain, build, enjoy beauty and achieve; to be recognized; to be protected or nurtured; to be autonomous; and many other needs.
- we help the client to love, to belong, to become free from inner conflict or to control.
- we present a solution to a problem.
- we surprise them with something extra.
- the product or the purchase event makes the client feel important or successful.
- the product or the purchase event makes the client feel competent.
- we differentiate our product from those of competitors along the lines important to the client.

- the client experiences the drama of the product or service in his or her life or in the lives of others.
- we show genuine concern for them as people.
- we are sincere in our dealings with them.
- they decide based on what makes them feel better.
- the act of purchasing has a certain level of excitement built in.

Why do you think advertising is focused almost exclusively on describing the benefits of a product, its purchase or its use? It's like the old sales maxim says: Benefits sell. And benefits are tied directly to consumer emotions, which fuel word of mouth.

I am not suggesting that you should attempt to tug at your clients' emotions all the time. To do this would be unethical and impractical. I am simply trying to raise your awareness of the power these emotions have in the business setting. Positive emotions help get your clients past the threshold of a "ho-hum" or merely adequate experience and into the arena of an experience they can talk about. Negative emotions get past the threshold of a good experience and into the ring for a fight.

Evaluating satisfaction is a personal process in which every client engages. You can't stop it. Like it or not, this is an inevitable part of conducting business. Why not create an experience that so overwhelms your clients with its positive side that small problems are insignificant?

Emotions During a Complaint

As a business manager, you have two responses when dealing with client emotions: the low road and the high road. The low-road response is to simply reflect the emotions of the client. When clients show happiness, you are happy. When they are excited, you get excited. This response can leave you energized at the end of the workday as you reflect on the positive emotions expressed to you by your clients. If, however, the emotions clients bring you are negative and directed toward you, it is just as easy to reflect back the same emotions. I've seen many angry customers come to businesses and vent their rage on the customer service personnel. Whether they leave with a solution to their complaint or not, the one taking care of them gets caught in the same web of emotion as the client.

Customer service personnel are trained to be in control of their emotions while serving unhappy clients. What I have seen is the eruption of emotion after the client leaves. The customer service person usually displays the same emotion observed in the client. In the unfortunate event that the customer service person does not control his or her emotions, the customer leaves even more angry, frustrated, hurt and disappointed. This mutual wallowing in misery leaves both you and your client out of control.

When clients complain about problems, they expect you to be in control, and not merely to reflect their displeasure. They want to see something tangible for their problem. They want you to take a position on the high road of finding a solution. The high-road response is to take the lead in establishing a positive emotional base to every client encounter. When you take the high road, your emotional state rubs off on everyone around you, including your employees, visitors, other clients, suppliers and, most important, your client. Taking the high road allows you to be in control and one mental step ahead of the client. It allows you to step back from clients' negative feelings and give them space to calm themselves down. Taking the high road helps you be unaffected by their emotions.

This does not mean that there is no place for anger, frustration and disappointment in dealing with complaining customers. These are very real emotions that arise when the client with negative attitudes pushes us beyond our point of reasonable patience.

Are feelings really positive or negative? I've used the terms as if these feelings are either good or bad, when in reality these are simply normal human experiences that exist. All feelings are good when they signal what is valuable to your customer. They are an important feedback message that you need to help you track your effectiveness.

So-called negative emotions signal a relationship that is temporarily blocked from being productive. They are a flag that the goals of one and probably both business parties are not being achieved. Negative emotions are indicators to both parties that all is not right. Ignoring these flags or belittling them will only complicate the situation. Acknowledging them, allowing them and identifying them does help as long as response is followed by a tangible solution to the problem.

Emotions such as frustration, disappointment and irritation are often hidden by consumers who use common courtesy to blind you to their real feelings. Consumers know how to shield others from knowing how they really feel. For this reason, I have suggested asking open-ended feedback questions when evaluating a consumer's experience. Asking a "yes or no" question allows consumers the luxury of hiding their true feelings. While it helps protect them from disclosing themselves, it gives you no practical help in improving your service.

The important negative emotions are

- anger,
- frustration,
- disappointment,
- confusion and
- hurt.

The important positive emotions are

- relief,
- satisfaction,
- gratitude,
- happiness and
- excitement.

*A*ction *A*genda

275. *Use the element of surprise.* Surprise your clients with something extra, something unexpected. Although it happens in many industries, it is unethical to make an arrangement with clients to bring in other clients in exchange for a payoff. Much more powerful is the pleasant surprise champion clients get after you learn they have extended your reputation in the community by sending someone else to you. If you are not careful, however, surprises can become your new client's expectations after he or she hears about the wonderful experience others had when purchasing from you. Make sure you reserve these surprises for your most loyal champion clients.

276. *Show it in action.* Practice using the actions of concern and avoid the actions of indifference. You communicate indifference when you

- change the subject while clients are speaking with you.
- give them a blank look.
- make no comment on something important to them.
- tell them your own negative feelings about the situation.
- tell them a story about something that happened to you.
- say, "I can't do anything about that."
- look away toward others when the client speaks directly to you.

277. *Be sincere.* Raise your awareness of how sincerity is communicated. The following are some examples of how to communicate sincerity:

- Look the client in the eye at all times.
- Do not allow interruptions to slow down the process with the client.
- Speak in a calm, controlled voice.
- Use a tone of voice that says, "I'm glad we are able to resolve this for you."
- Use a lower-pitched voice.
- Use facial expressions that show you understand what they feel. (Smiling at the wrong time can mean that you think their complaint is a joke.)
- Smile at the completion of the conversation when resolution is achieved.
- Thank them for bringing their complaint to you.

278. *Train clients how to get the most for their money.* Many clients fear that they will be hooked into a continual dependence on you for your services. Training your clients how to carry on without you will build more trust. This will be something remarkable to associates and business friends. Champion clients want to learn more so they can fulfill their role as opinion leaders. Additional training will only make it easier for them to refer others to you for advice.

279. *Let happy customers show their satisfaction to others.* Structure a meeting between satisfied clients and potential clients so that the prospective clients can see the emotions of real people who purchased from you. Invite your champion clients to a seminar you present and have them say something about their experience. Introduce them to seminar participants and watch the prospective clients flock to them after the seminar to ask them how they feel about your services. Develop a "users' group" and invite champions and prospective clients to attend.

280. *Use humor carefully.*   Humor, if used tastefully, triggers positive emotions. Interview your satisfied clients and ask for the human interest elements that show examples of how your products helped them work through a humorous situation. By itself, humor is not a good persuader. Linked with identifiable needs and benefits, however, it can be a sign that you have triggered some positive emotions. Stories (which you get approval to use) in which humor is prominently featured communicate with prospective clients that others appreciate your products.

281. *Find out what excites you.*   Talk to your champions about these things and get their responses, both verbal and nonverbal. Record yourself on videotape as you tell a prospective client about the features and benefits of your service. Then watch the tape to observe the consistency between your verbal and nonverbal messages. Make improvements so that you are conveying positive emotions throughout your presentations.

282. *Explore others' enthusiasm.*   Find existing clients who tend to exhibit higher-than-average enthusiasm about your product. Interview them to capture the exact phrases and tone of voice they use to describe what you sell. Ask specifically what makes them so enthusiastic. Obtain permission to borrow their phrases and words to describe your product to others.

283. *Suggest referrals.*   Say something like the following: "My reputation is the most valuable professional resource I possess in this community. I know that you have had a good experience with my services. If you have an opportunity to make a suggestion to someone looking for the kinds of services I provide, would you be willing to suggest me?"

284. *Show by example.*   Relate to your champion clients how things worked for people who purchased your service. Dramatizing the experience involves others in the process of feeling and thinking about their own reaction to your service. Maintain the focus on problem solving. The human interest story is the backbone of many grapevine marketing successes. When telling a story about something real that happened to another client, be sure to

- tell the truth.
- avoid embellishing the story with your own interpretation of the feelings involved.
- help clients draw conclusions about the benefits for them; however, let them draw their own conclusions about the emotional impact of the event. Most people have some ability to empathize with others in a similar situation.
- avoid using emotion for emotion's sake. This is not only unethical, it also can backfire on you by offending the one hearing the story.
- tell the significance (the benefit) to the client as it was told to you. Quote your champions when describing the benefits of your products.
- avoid breaking confidences. Get permission to use clients' names or statements.

A variation is printing up written versions of one or two stories. First get permission from champions to use their story. Show them a copy of what you write before you start using it. Give your champions copies of these stories and ask them to pass them out to their friends or associates. You can give them to new clients.

285. *Let them say it.*   Give your champion clients a chance to tell you the story illustrating what is so important about your service. Always conduct a follow-up interview a few days or weeks after the completion of the transaction. If you believe you have done something remarkable for them and you are not getting the emotional response you would expect, ask them a few questions, such as the following:

- How has this event changed your work?
- How do you feel about what has happened?
- What was the most important aspect of this service to you and your company?

Don't drag out the interview. Give positive feedback and acknowledgment as you hear the story. Ask them for permission to use the story in discussing your services with others. Ask if they know anyone who should hear the story. Allowing your clients the chance to tell you the story helps to crystallize the meaning and the details in their own mind. It gives them practice telling others. Talking about your service to someone else makes your champions' opinion of you stronger than if they kept silent. Through a discussion with you, they will refine their own words to more accurately describe what your service means. They will hear you reflect on what they say and will likely incorporate your reflections the next time they talk about your service.

286. *Make benefits clear.* If you are not sure which benefits are the most important to customers, have discussions with current satisfied clients. Then have a brainstorming session in your office to make sure you are not missing something important.

287. *Be cautious.* Be careful if you use a celebrity to give a testimonial. It is not lawful to use a celebrity to assert a claim they are not qualified to make. Make sure you are not in violation of Federal Trade Commission regulations or state or federal antitrust laws. This suggestion is not meant as legal advice. Get expert advice on this issue from legal counsel to minimize the risk of violating any laws.

288. *Be congruous.* If you use a celebrity, make sure there is a link between what that person stands for in the minds of consumers and what buying, using or possessing your product means. When the celebrity is incongruous with the product, it will result in failure and a waste of your financial resources. It is a good idea to test the concept of a celebrity with your champion customers before you spend any endorsement money. Ask them what potential celebrities represent, what they symbolize in culture, and what people like and dislike about them. Also ask these champions in what ways your product is similar or dissimilar to a celebrity you are considering.

289. *Learn the reason behind the emotion.*   Avoid focusing exclusively on the emotions rather than on what is behind them. The reasons your champion clients get excited is ultimately more important than the fact that they get excited. Knowing the reasons for their feelings will help you duplicate the experience for other customers.

290. *Select the endorsement carefully.*   If your product or service carries some perceived psychological or social risk of purchase or ownership, a celebrity may be your best choice. This may also be the case when you target a selected segment to whom celebrities are significant, such as youth or product enthusiasts. When your product carries a perceived complexity or physical risk, choose an expert as a spokesperson. Typical consumers can be used for endorsement of products with low perceived risk.

*P*rofiles Of *S*uccess

Seven Crown Resorts
Irvine, California

Business Profile: Seven Crown Resorts offers a variety of houseboat vacation packages in the western states.

Word-of-Mouth Tactics: Karen Lippe, director of marketing and sales, tries to build loyal customers. She thinks that this is one of the best ways to build word of mouth. The more loyal a customer is, the more likely it is that he or she will tell others about the great experience possible with Seven Crown Resorts. When a family has a great experience, they usually want to share that experience with friends during the next vacation. "We try to inspire word of mouth with the complete package that customers buy," Karen says. It must be working.

Seven Crown Resorts combines the skills of computer-aided direct marketing with good service. To encourage repeat business, the company offers a variety of incentives, including early-reservation discounts and bonuses. She tracks the dollar value that repeat customers represent as well as their buying history. Using this database, she mails out special offers to repeat customers encouraging them to make reservations. When customers call, trained reservation agents help them decide what type of vacation will best meet their needs.

During one direct mail campaign, repeat customers were given the option of coming to the houseboat the evening before their trip was to begin so that they could spend the night on board. The "Free Early Board" program was offered to families reserving (with the required deposit) a houseboat by a certain date.

Results: In 1992, 39 percent of Seven Crown Resorts customers were repeat customers. With a consistent direct-marketing program and refined services, the proportion had grown to 46 percent two years later and it continues to climb. Seventeen percent of 1994 revenue was generated from word-of-mouth promotion. *(Used by permission from Seven Crown Resorts)*

Chapter 13

*C*reating and Promoting a Visible Code of Conduct

*"*When men speak ill of thee, so live that nobody will believe them.*"*

— *Plato*

*"*The only time people dislike gossip is when you gossip about them.*"*

— *Will Rogers*

*E*very year thousands of professionals are convicted of white-collar crimes like bribery, theft, fraud, embezzlement, kickbacks, deception and other forms of unethical behavior. Somewhere along the way, many of these professionals lost sight of why they were in business to begin with: to serve for the good of others. Many let the focus on self-interest overshadow everything they were trying to accomplish. In an attempt to sustain a profitable enterprise (the other reason for being in business), they let themselves go to the extreme of doing harm. In some cases, the stories of these unsavory behaviors are sensationalized in the media, resulting in social isolation.

Companies are criticized for

- planning obsolescence.
- differentiating solely on advertising hype.
- using too much packaging.
- creating unsafe products.
- defrauding suppliers and organizational buyers.
- being wasteful.
- deceiving children and youth.
- refusing to clear up ambiguity regarding quality.
- exaggerating the message about the benefits.
- attempting to persuade using appeals to human emotion.

And can you blame the critics? There are enough abuses of marketing power to go around for all major industries.

Some business managers, while maintaining high personal standards of conduct outside of work, feel pressured to lower their professional conduct because of the demands of business. In an international survey covering hundreds of business managers from 16 countries, researchers found that over 50 percent of these leaders felt conflict between what the company wanted and their own moral standards. Concealment of the truth, falsification of information, bribes, inappropriate gifts and irregular payments are some of the most common activities these managers feel pressured to perform to help their businesses meet their objectives.

Renewed interest in ethical conduct is bringing spiritual values back to business. Consumers and industry watchers are concerned that the excesses of the previous decades have left us void of moral standards. These are the times to revisit ethics and establish our moral roots. In my opinion, when word of mouth is emphasized more often, higher ethical standards will prevail.

Your Responsibilities Using Word of Mouth

As with any promotion tactic, word-of-mouth marketing carries with it certain responsibilities for high-level ethical behavior. And, like any business practice, word of mouth carries risks of abuse.

I have mentioned more than once the importance of saying thank you in appropriate ways to show your opinion leaders how much you appreciate their referrals. Taken too far, however, this kind of activity can be abused and manipulative. I urge you to avoid manipulating people to achieve your own business goals.

Word-of-mouth marketing, when practiced consistently, can have a binding effect between you and your target market. First, your champion customers refer others to you expecting that you will provide their friends with the same good service and high-quality products that they received.

Second, as your reputation is spread throughout the community, it sets up expectations on the part of people who are not even in your target market. This implicit contract is ratified every time a champion customer goes out and talks about you to others. Watch that you continue to fulfill this obligation, and when you cannot fulfill it, be sure that you make amends quickly and painlessly for those affected.

Several other aspects of word-of-mouth marketing should be studied to minimize the risk of getting off the high road of a good reputation. Among them are the following:

1. Avoid taking the words of well-meaning champion clients out of context when using them as an endorsement. It may come back to haunt you later.

2. If you give away samples, make it crystal-clear to the recipients that they are not obligated to do anything with the product except enjoy it. Even if you ask them to try it and to discuss the product with their friends, make it clear that they are under no obligation to do so.

3. If you promote a product that you know causes harm to others (even if you have a group of champions pushing it for you), you have an obligation to withdraw the product from the market.

4. When you offer a product you are unwilling to support with after-the-sale service, you are creating an expectation that you will not fulfill. When selling a product, you are, in my opinion, obligated to inform consumers that they should or should not expect a certain level of after-the-sale service from you. If you offer service, provide it. Offering a sham for service is just another form of deception.

5. A large portion of this book is devoted to the issue of developing your reputation. I realize that you cannot control what others say about you and that this word-of-mouth dynamic is, to a large extent, the fire behind your reputation. However, if you intentionally try to promote a reputation that is a half truth, your ethical standard is suspect. For this and other reasons, you should avoid making public claims about your ability to give excellent service until your service matches the claim. If you bring in new champion-type customers with advertising that claims you have high quality when you don't, you will set up a storm of negative word of mouth. In short, make sure there is substance behind the image. Focusing on reputation at the expense of substantive service for consumers is misspent energy.

6. If giving any kind of a gift makes you feel like you are bribing champions, avoid doing it. I recommend that you follow closely what you believe to be right.

7. If you have a contest in your store to gather names of potential opinion leaders, make sure you clearly state the rules of the game so there are no misunderstandings. Inform consumers about your purpose in the contest—that you want to get their names and addresses to communicate with them regarding other products and services you offer.

8. When you anticipate a delay in fulfilling any consumer request for service, you should inform the consumer. People appreciate knowing about delays.

9. Refund policies should be made clear to customers at the time of purchase. When a consumer asks for a refund to which he or she is entitled, fulfill the request quickly. If you give the customer a free trial offer with no obligations, pay up quickly when you get returns.

10. Don't give a product to consumers without their permission and expect that they will pay for it. If you use such a tactic, explain clearly how customers can terminate the relationship with full refunds and no further obligations.

11. If you use guarantees, state the terms clearly, in plain English and in large print. Consult with your attorney regarding the use of specific wording, but make the policy user-friendly by keeping it simple to understand.

12. If you use testimonials from champions, make sure they are bona fide users of your products and services. Get written permission to use their statements, and keep such permissions in your files.

13. When you make price comparisons with competitors, be sure they are factual and verifiable. Price is always a hot topic of discussion when opinion leaders talk. Resist the urge to overstate the truth.

14. If you describe a product in writing, in a photo or on videotape (this goes for services as well), make sure the representation is accurate and not distorted to deceive the consumer into thinking the product is something other than what it actually is.

The community of consumers is the group that ultimately gives you permission to conduct business. When you decide to establish a business, you are, in essence, agreeing to the minimum standards of conduct as set by the community. Whether you like it or not, the community of customers you serve senses what is right and wrong. Nothing you do escapes the watchful eyes of the community judges who are looking to see whether your work is ethical. If you violate a standard of conduct, you pay the price with an injured reputation. The result: Negative word of mouth spreads like wildfires. In the final analysis, consumers always have public recourse for dissatisfying purchasing experiences they have had with unethical business owners.

There is a practical reason for conducting your affairs ethically. When a client or a member of the public interacts with you, you represent your entire company. You *are* the company. If your conduct is less than acceptable to the other person, you may have started negative word of mouth. If what you do is really controversial, you may have to close up shop and leave town.

A Code of Conduct

I surveyed several professional codes of conduct and found many common elements that, when followed, will promote a positive reputation. Based on the codes of conduct I have studied, I have chosen the following three arenas in which your conduct influences word of mouth:

1. Conduct with the public and with prospective clients

   - Avoid discrimination on the basis of race, color, gender, age or nationality.
   - Avoid making false or misleading statements about your abilities or about the projected results of your work. Do not make promises you cannot fulfill.
   - Disclose all relationships with others who have any interests in your work and who could influence you in any way.
   - Disclose all potential conflicts of interest to potential clients.
   - Avoid false advertising.
   - Avoid high-pressure, manipulative or deceptive sales tactics.

- Do not manipulate the availability of your service or products for the purpose of exploitation.
- Do not use coercion to achieve sales.
- Do not fix prices or otherwise restrain trade.
- Avoid attempting to sell under the guise of conducting research.
- Obey all federal, state and local laws governing your profession and civil behavior.
- Do not disregard the rights of others. Do unto others as you would have them do unto you.

2. Conduct with clients

- Do not knowingly cause harm to another person or organization.
- Do the best job and offer the best quality you can.
- Make genuine good-faith efforts to fulfill all your commitments and promises to clients.
- Maintain information about clients in strict confidence, disclosing to others only that for which the client expressly gives permission.
- Offer to perform professional services only when you or those you employ are qualified by training, education or experience.
- Do not assist a client in engaging in fraudulent or illegal actions. Do not engage in fraudulent or illegal actions yourself.
- Avoid attempting to influence public officials with respect to services you perform or products you sell to any client.
- Do not try to take credit for a job someone else has done for your client.
- Disclose to clients all known risks associated with your services.
- Use your knowledge and skill for the advancement of human welfare.

3. Conduct with competitors and others in your industry

- Do not make comparisons with any competitor that cannot be backed up with factual evidence.
- Do not falsely or maliciously discredit the reputation of a competitor.

- Do not misrepresent a competitor to a prospective client.
- Act professionally toward competitors at all times.
- Use fair pricing methods.
- Do not act in ways that bring dishonor on your profession.
- Actively support and honor the code of ethics in your profession or industry.
- Avoid trying to supplant another professional in a particular job after he or she has been awarded a contract.
- Avoid using a salaried position to gain an unfair competitive advantage over other professionals.
- Don't review the work of another professional for the same client except with the knowledge of the other professional, unless the contract between that professional and the client has been terminated.

Other Ethical Issues To Consider

Free-enterprise systems are built on the assumption that all parties to a business exchange wish to get something of higher value than they possess before the exchange. Consumers understand that you manage a business relationship and that you do not owe them anything more than fair exchanges of value. You have no business obligation to contribute to their favorite charity or to help them fix a flat tire.

Consumers also recognize that you are in business to make a profit. However, many consumers share a concern that what they bring to the exchange is used unfairly for profits of questionable magnitudes. Buyers are wary when they believe a business takes advantage of others. When a business owner goes out of his or her way to give something extra and unexpected, some consumers are ecstatic, while others look for "the catch." Given the prevalence of consumer attitudes toward businesses, consider how you may be able to differentiate yourself from competitors solely on the basis of honesty, fairness and openness. Think of the powerful messages champion customers tell when they realize you have a genuine interest in ethical conduct.

If your company, through a mistake, contributes to social harm in some way, you have an obligation to alleviate the consequences. Just as individual citizens have a responsibility to stay involved in the larger issues faced by society, so do companies. Count the social costs of doing business before you enter into new ventures. In doing so, you are taking this larger responsibility seriously. And, as your motive to provide service to others grows, you will do well as you seek to do good.

Business by its very nature is a social activity. As a professional, you cannot escape the social implications of your business policies. Business professionals cannot afford the luxury of making excuses for betraying the public trust. Business is too close to society for this.

Promoting Positive Word of Mouth

As suggested earlier, business ethics have a practical dimension. It is typically less expensive to prevent ethical problems from surfacing than it is to pay for cleaning up after ethical blunders. Also, sustaining a reputation for being ethical in all your affairs translates into increased sales and higher profits.

*A*ction *A*genda

291. *If you believe that you have been acting inappropriately, make an immediate correction of your actions.*

292. *Watch your private life.* A code of ethics is just the beginning, a bare minimum that allows you on the playing field of competition. Promoting positive word of mouth is accomplished by exceeding the bare minimum in highly visible, as well as very private, ways. You may say, "What I do in my private life is my business." Technically, you may be correct. As a business professional, however, you never have the luxury of acting in ways contrary to your professional code of ethics. Remember the important principle of word of mouth: People talk. Therefore, your private life is filled with opportunities to build a positive reputation. Living a life of high personal morals when no one seems to be watching is your best defense against negative rumors.

293. Avoid controversial relations with individuals of the opposite gender. Perceived sexual improprieties or rumors about such travel via word of mouth faster than almost any other type of story.

294. Stay close to your champions. Talk to your champion clients about ethical practices. Ask them to give you feedback regarding anything, no matter how small or insignificant, that they have ever felt uncomfortable about when dealing with your company. Log their suggestions and feedback. When gathering this information, avoid a defensive posture. Simply listen and try to understand what they are feeling. You will have ample opportunity later to defend your past actions in the privacy of your office.

295. Go for value. Emphasize your champion clients' values. If you focus on the values they hold dear, you will be at less risk of engaging in unethical behavior.

296. Increase consumer choice. Increase the range of choices you offer clients, as well as their ability to choose. When you restrict choice, you control the relationship. Too much restriction can lead to unethical actions.

297. Emphasize voluntary consumer action. Recognize the voluntary actions of your customers by thanking them for the work they do in supporting your reputation.

Profiles Of Success

Anderson Construction
Westminster, Massachusetts

Business Profile: Builder of custom homes and buildings.

Word-of-Mouth Tactics: Kim Anderson, owner of Anderson Construction, doesn't do any paid advertising. He believes it is the product that convinces customers to tell their friends about his work. He starts by helping the customer to understand both short-term and long-term property needs. He refuses to make snap judgments about what he should do for customers. Anderson typically has more than a perfunctory conversation with new customers. He works at developing a relationship that will last a long time. And, during the project, he keeps customers informed of the progress his crew is making.

When customers want to participate in some phase of the project, Anderson encourages their involvement. "This personal involvement lets them see the level of quality that is built into the property from the ground up," says Anderson. Anderson even educates customers about how to improve the quality of their own work through participation in the project. This increases the enthusiasm with which customers talk about his work to their friends and family. Sometimes customers are so committed to making a recommendation that they accompany Anderson to visit one of their friends who needs a builder.

When Anderson gets a new customer, he always makes a telephone call to the referring customer. Then he makes a point of doing a favor for this person to let him or her know he appreciates the support.

Kim Anderson is aware that even when he is not working for one of his customers, he can generate referrals. Kim enjoys training and showing Morgan horses in his spare time. One day, when he was at a horse show warming up his show horses, another trainer watched the way Kim handled the beautiful animals. This observant trainer had heard that Kim was a builder. After watching Kim work with the horses, the other trainer telephoned someone who was looking for a qualified builder. This trainer later said that he recommended Anderson believing that if he could handle Morgan horses with such remarkable quality, he must manage his construction work the same way.

Results: One hundred percent of Anderson Construction customers come by referral from other customers and business associates who know Anderson's work. *(Used by permission from Anderson Construction)*

Chapter 14

*T*urning Your Customers into Champions

"Give them quality. That's the best kind of advertising."

— *Milton S. Hershey*

"Associate with men of good quality if you esteem your own reputation; for it is better to be alone than in bad company."

— *George Washington*

*E*very customer you serve is a potential champion. In your opinion, some people may not fit the profile of the typical opinion leader. However, if these customers have the opportunity to speak about you only one time to just one other person, they fulfill the role of opinion leader for that person. That one time may be their shining moment as a champion, and it is a moment you cannot afford to overlook. By giving excellent service at each moment of truth, you can make all your customers champions.

90+ Questions That Help You See Your Business from Your Customer's Perspective

Here are some situations and issues in which your customers face what, for you, are moments of truth. Each represents an opportunity to provide excellent service and create a positive reputation. However, each also represents a corresponding risk of creating dissatisfaction if the experience does not meet the customer's expectations.

The following questions are written as if addressed to one of your customers. How will each and every customer be able to answer these questions?

Before the First Contact with the Company

1. Did you have information (phone number, location, hours of availability, etc.) about how to contact our business?
2. Did the referring person give you adequate information that added to your positive expectations? (This would include information on background, experience, office hours, location, parking, names of personnel who can help, etc.)
3. Have you heard about our company or our work from friends, family members, directories or other professionals? What kind of reputation do we have?

Calling for Information

4. Did you have the correct telephone number?
5. Was the call answered promptly?
6. Was the call answered courteously?
7. Was the person who answered competent?
8. Were you put on hold? If so, for how long?
9. Was the person you spoke with willing to help?
10. Did he or she understand what you needed?
11. If your call was transferred, did it get transferred to the correct person the first time?
12. Did you hear negative phrases, such as "I don't know," "That's not my job" or "You'll have to ask the company president about that yourself"?
13. If an answering service took the call, did they ask for pertinent information and give you helpful information?
14. Did you receive a callback soon after employees were scheduled to return to the office?
15. How accessible was the appointment time to you? Were the time of day and day of the week convenient?
16. How many days did you have to wait for the appointment?
17. Were you informed about the products and services our company offers?
18. Were you told what information would be needed when you came for the appointment?
19. Were you informed about a cancellation policy?

20. Did the person you spoke with offer directions on how to get to our company?
21. Were you informed of any special issues, such as parking, the best times to come and whom to ask for when you arrived?
22. Did our personnel understand what you needed from our company?

Getting to Your Company

23. Were the directions correct and written in language you could easily follow?
24. Did you locate our business quickly?
25. Was our location convenient to your home or place of employment?
26. Could you find the front door easily?
27. Was there adequate parking?
28. Did you feel safe parking and walking to the entrance?

The Welcoming Process

29. Were you greeted within 20 seconds of your arrival?
30. Did the person who greeted you introduce himself or herself by name, clearly and distinctly? Did that person ask for your name?
31. Were you greeted courteously and warmly?
32. Was the welcoming staff member willing to help?
33. Were you helped with the process, or were you left on your own?
34. Did you know what to do next and where to find help?
35. Were you informed what to do next and where to go?
36. Did you understand the purpose of any forms you were asked to complete?
37. Did the personnel you met seem sympathetic?
38. Were you confused about anything relating to our company?
39. How long did you wait for help?
40. Did other customers seem satisfied?
41. Did help arrive quickly?
42. Were you comfortable while you waited?
43. Was our business clean and free of offensive odors?
44. Were all the staff members eager to help?

45. Were staff members concerned about your privacy?
46. Were staff members sensitive to any special needs you have?
47. Were you briefed about what to expect as a result of your visit?
48. Were attitudes toward other customers (in person and on the telephone) positive?
49. Was your purchase process error-free the first time?
50. Were you spoken to by name by any of our personnel?
51. Was the atmosphere of our company calm?
52. Were any delays explained to you in terms that were specific and sensible?

Service

53. Did you get to meet someone in authority?
54. Was this person courteous and personable?
55. Did this person seem to be in a hurry?
56. Was your contact with this person longer or shorter than you expected?
57. Did you have enough time with the key person in our company?
58. Did you feel safe while making your purchase from our company?
59. Were you informed about any future products or services or the capabilities of our services that you would need later?
60. Were you informed about what to do next?
61. Did our equipment appear to function correctly the first time?
62. Were all transactions performed correctly the first time?
63. Were you able to select the appropriate product or service to meet your needs?
64. If you had additional questions about our products or services, were they answered adequately and courteously?

Making Financial Arrangements

65. Did you discuss sensitive financial arrangements in private?
66. Did you understand payment policies and the reasons for those policies?
67. Did you feel like a valued customer during the financial discussions?

68. Were you informed about the various options for payment?
69. Were these instructions clear to you?

Leaving Your Business

70. What was your overall level of satisfaction with our services?
71. What was your level of confidence in the services performed?
72. Did you finish with your purchase when you expected?
73. Could you find your car easily?
74. Did you feel safe walking from the office to your car?
75. If you left by taxi or public transportation, did someone help you with arrangements?

Follow-up

76. Did someone call you after your purchase to get feedback?
77. Did the product or service "work" correctly the first time?
78. Were you offered recommendations about what to do next?
79. Did the staff seem to be concerned about how satisfied you were with the service?
80. Were you encouraged to follow through on any special instructions given by the person in charge?
81. Were you given adequate information about any additional services that were recommended?
82. Did you receive the information you needed to access the customer service department?
83. Were you addressed by name?
84. Did the staff person introduce himself or herself by name?
85. Was the financial statement correct?
86. Did you receive all the information that was promised?
87. Do you feel like a valued customer?
88. Would you recommend the company to a friend?
89. Do you feel good enough about the service that you would tell someone else how good it was? Was the service adequate, or was it exceptional?
90. If you had a complaint, did the first person you talk to have a solution, or did you get bounced from person to person?
91. Did the office staff members seem to be aware of your feelings?

92. What were your first impressions?
93. Would you return to this company for additional products or services?

Profiles Of Success

Malcolm Smith Motor Sports
Riverside, California

Business Profile: Malcolm Smith Motor Sports sells motorcycles, motorcycle accessories, personal watercraft and sportswear for motor sports. The company also offers comprehensive motorcycle and watercraft repair services.

Word-of-Mouth Tactics: To business owner Malcolm Smith, himself a world champion off-road cyclist, word of mouth starts with offering the same high level of service to everyone who comes into the store. "You cannot accurately judge from a person's appearance whether or not the person will be a qualified buyer and a spokesman for you," says Smith. The other principle that Smith emphasizes with his employees is the word-of-mouth golden rule: "Treat customers like you would want to be treated if you had recommended the store to others."

Off-road motorcycle customers form their own community, which provides a natural setting for word of mouth. They talk about cycles and riding, where to find quality products and where to get good service for their equipment. Malcolm Smith taps into the power of this goldmine by having his sales staff ask all new customers who referred them to the store. When a salesman identifies the referring customer, Smith often sends a little something to this individual, along with a thank-you note.

One day a tour bus rolled up to Malcolm Smith Motor Sports carrying a load of touring motorcycle enthusiasts from Japan. The tourists had spotted the store and asked the bus driver to stop and let them shop in the store. Because of the positive experience the tourists enjoyed, the bus driver told other tour bus drivers about the company, and they started bringing tourists to the store. When asked why they continue to do this, bus drivers usually say that it is the quality sales service the store employees give to foreign tourists. If he is in the store, Malcolm Smith makes it a point to meet the tour bus drivers and acknowledge their support with a baseball cap or some other small token of appreciation.

Results: Word of mouth accounts for about 50 percent of all first-time customers to Malcolm Smith Motor Sports. It is no surprise that the majority of customers become repeat customers. *(Used by permission from Malcolm Smith Motor Sports)*

Chapter *15*

*S*taying Ahead

*"*A man is always stronger while making a reputation than he is after it is made.*"*

—*Josh Billings*

*W*ord-of-mouth marketing requires an ongoing commitment to improve your reputation if you expect results to continue. It also requires a high degree of involvement from your staff. The only way to ensure a high level of commitment over time is through continued learning.

Left alone over time, word-of-mouth marketing will go from good to adequate, to bad, to worse as awareness and skills deteriorate. Each new employee might not have the level of interpersonal skills you desire. New equipment will be purchased, requiring new skills. Regulatory agencies may require new procedures. Old habits that place your reputation at risk may surface as stress increases. Without training, your company will slide into a state of confusion. A negative reputation will usually follow.

I recently surveyed the successful customer service programs of 50 leading American companies. One of the common threads was the high priority these companies placed on training. Employees at these firms know that they will have to participate in continual training with respect to word-of-mouth marketing. When the training is effective, employees work better, get positive feedback from clients, complain less and become more enthusiastic. In other words, not only do well-trained employees enhance the company's reputation, they also have higher morale.

Let's assume you have instituted a training program for word-of-mouth marketing. It's been two months now since you got everyone interested in the program. You get to work one morning and realize that the old habits are back; you are letting important marketing details slip through the cracks. You listen in on a conversation between an employee and a customer and hear excuses instead of solutions. Customers at the reception window begin complaining about mistakes, but you do not see anyone in the customer service department actively looking for ways to eliminate these problems. You notice that the only follow-up communication your office has with customers occurs when there are problems to solve. Customers leave the business anxious, frustrated or angry.

It's time for a refresher course to build habits that bolster your reputation. Those habits include

- honesty.
- positive communication with customers between visits.
- accepting responsibility for mistakes and taking immediate action to correct them.
- including customers in major office transitions.
- showing gratitude.
- communicating personally with customers.
- being available.
- confusion-free business operations.

What should be next on the training course schedule? The Action Agenda offers ideas to draw from as you develop an ongoing training program. The suggestions enable you to develop and conduct a training program on your own, avoiding the need to hire an outside consultant. You can do the research, organize the program, present training sessions, develop practice skills and evaluate the results. Think of it as a repeating course in operational skills that every staff member is expected to participate in, including yourself.

If you believe that training is for staff members only, because they seem to be responsible for most of the problems with customers, you will torpedo your word-of-mouth marketing program. The employees will go home and say to their families, "The boss expects us to go through all these stupid training programs, but he doesn't attend himself. He's the one who really needs the training." When you participate in the training with your employees, you indicate that you take word-of-mouth marketing seriously. This motivates staff members to be serious about the program. It also shows that you are not above learning how to improve your customer skills and that everyone is expected to participate. In addition, it can reduce the risk of complaints by 100 percent.

*A*ction *A*genda

298. *Train yourself and your supervisors to identify problems.* Your employees have the power to generate positive feelings and consumer confidence. They also have the power to create concern, irritation and a host of other problems that result in negative word of mouth. I was on an airplane once and heard a flight attendant loudly proclaiming his frustration at having to wait three hours to get on the flight so he could transfer to another city. He was further angered because he had to sit on one of the uncomfortable seats that the working flight attendants use during takeoff and landing. The customers for several rows around heard him exclaim that he wished the airline would go bankrupt soon. The other flight attendants bought in to his frustration and even encouraged him to vent his anger. Are your employees on the verge of creating this type of scene? Here are some flags that indicate your employees may be causing negative word of mouth.

- *You ask your employees how things are and they don't tell you anything.* If they just say "everything is fine," you are not getting the message. And by the time you do get the message, it could be too late. If this is the response you get, begin monitoring yourself to see if you respond defensively when problems are brought to your attention. Defensive listening creates mistrust and throws up barriers to communication. Begin listening without defensiveness.

- *If the surface seems to be smooth when customers are served but chaotic behind the scenes, you have a problem.* Your employees are just a breath away from getting involved with a potentially negative word-of-mouth situation. If you find that one or two staff members repeatedly have to solve problems, you either have problems with your company structure or below-the-surface personnel conflicts. If this sounds like your organization, get more involved with the nitty-gritty operational details to identify the underlying causes of the chaos. Then make the appropriate changes.

- *You hear faint rumblings that indicate your employees are not happy.* Unhappiness is exhibited when employees frequently call in sick or show up late for work. Begin active listening to find out what the problems are. Encourage employees to consider changes they can make on their own, but stay involved in the process. For larger problems that employees are unable to solve, do your best to find solutions.

- *The worst case is when you find that employees are verbally expressing their frustration or anger either in front of customers or directly to customers.* This situation needs immediate action. The process of identifying the problem and negotiating a solution should be swift. In some cases, the employee disciplinary process should be initiated. Let your employees know that this type of behavior will not be tolerated, no matter how difficult the problem is.

299. *Train your staff in telephone skills.*   I often hear the telephone answered with a simple "Hello" when I call a business. It would be nice to know to whom I am speaking. It would be nice to know that the person answering the phone is interested in talking to me. The other telephone phrase I hear a lot from customer service is "What is your problem?" I know the receptionist is trying to get to the root of the issue quickly, but the question can leave the caller feeling as if he or she has been an inconvenience to the business. I'm sure you get the idea of what the problem is. Your employees should answer the phone quickly, usually within three rings, and identify your office and themselves by name. They should speak distinctly even when they are in a hurry to pick up other lines.

300. *Use the "telephone tag game" to improve telephone-answering skills.*   For these simple drills, prepare a list of questions or complaints that require the staff to practice positive skills. The more difficult, the better, as the practice will increase the confidence of the staff in solving telephone problems. The questions are written down on small note cards or papers and shuffled. Have all participants seated in a circle. Deal one card to each staff member and place the remaining cards in a stack face down on the table. The person to the left of the dealer reads his or her card to any staff member in the circle. That person's task is to think of a positive response immediately. If he or she cannot think of a positive response, anyone in the circle may answer. Then others who have alternate responses are allowed to contribute their ideas. Play passes to the next person to the left, and so on until everyone has a chance to both read and respond to a card. If you want to keep score, develop a simple point system for acceptable answers. One round each staff meeting may be sufficient for skill development to reach the level you desire. Following are some sample questions or complaints to write on the cards.

- "May I speak with _____[the name of a staff member]?"
- "How can I get to _____[the name of a business across town that you rarely refer clients to for services] from my house?"
- "Why didn't I get my _____[product] back today?"
- "Why did you bill me twice for _____?"
- "I already paid for the product when I was in your store. Now I get a bill for it. Can you do something about this?"
- "I know your boss is with a customer, but I want to talk to her now."
- "Can I change my appointment to Monday evening?"
- "I forgot how I'm supposed to use this product. What do I do?"
- "Can you ask the manager not to charge me so much? I don't think I can pay the whole amount."
- "I don't have any way to get to your office for my appointment. Can you help me find a ride?"
- "Tell your boss that John called."
- Write down some of the complaints and questions you hear from your customers and add them to your cards.

Unacceptable responses include phrases such as "I don't know," "No" (when it begins a sentence), "You have to ask the owner," "That's not my job," "I just work here; call back in the afternoon," "We don't have that," "The person who knows that isn't here now," "I don't know when he is coming in" and "I'm not sure."

301. *Create a policies and procedures manual.* Provide all employees with job descriptions and policies so that no one will ever have to say "I don't know" to a customer again. If you don't have an office policies and procedures manual, develop one immediately and make sure each employee reads and understands every page. It is best to design it for a three-ring binder so you can make page revisions without revising the whole document. Think of your policies and procedures manual as a word-of-mouth marketing safety manual.

302. *Conduct technical skill review sessions.* At each staff meeting, take one piece of office equipment and have a five-minute refresher on how it is to be used. During the training, emphasize the importance of getting it right the first time. Remind staff members to avoid letting their frustrations show if the equipment doesn't work correctly. Your staff members should be proficient in the use of the following:

- Telephone system (Many customers become frustrated because they get cut off or their calls are transferred to the wrong extension.)
- Computer scheduling software
- Fax machine
- Charge card machines
- Reception room equipment (television, VCR, fish tanks, lamps, etc.)

303. *Cross-train employees in job responsibilities.* Why is it important for several people to know how to serve a customer, answer questions about office policies and procedures, and do other tasks that involve customer service? You never know when the person designated to handle these tasks will be unavailable when a customer arrives. Cross-training decreases office confusion, builds respect among employees and gives everyone a stake in the outcome.

304. *Engage your customers in error-free treasure hunting.* This is a good way to identify areas for office improvement. It can raise the awareness of all employees with respect to the procedures most at risk for errors. It is also a way to conduct problem-solving sessions to correct errors in customer service. This training exercise helps get rid of old ways of thinking and old ideas, such as "everyone makes mistakes" and "let someone else take care of it." Tell your customers you are running a promotion aimed at developing an error-free company, and ask for their assistance in identifying errors. See how enthusiastically they respond to help you.

305. *Plan for the worst.*   I know this sounds negative, but it is a valuable tool when major office disasters occur. If you have not mentally reviewed worst-case scenarios ahead of time, you and your customers are in for a rude awakening. For example, what will you do when your computer system crashes? Will you be able to answer customer inquiries, schedule appointments, complete financial transactions, send out reminder notices and continue your word-of-mouth marketing program? Or will you just use the computer as an excuse every time a customer calls with a problem? What will your employees do if there is a major disaster and you have customers in the office? What will you do for your customers? What if a violent or verbally abusive customer comes in and disrupts the whole office? What will you do and say? Think about it. These scenarios represent public relations nightmares. Without a disaster plan in place, you are at risk.

306. *Make sure your employees know the business.*   Take a few minutes at a staff meeting to inform all the personnel about the services you offer. This keeps them from having to say "I don't know" to customers. It also keeps them alert for additional ways to be of service. If you don't have a written list of all the services you provide, make one and give everybody a copy.

307. *Look at moments of truth or consequences.*   During a staff meeting, pick a few of the moments of truth from Chapter 8 and ask your staff, "What are the consequences if our customers are dissatisfied with this moment of truth? How can we make them satisfied today?"

308. *Focus on solving problems faster.*   Here is an area where you can really overwhelm customers. If you jump on a problem the moment it is brought to your attention and solve it so fast that the customer's head is swimming, he or she is not likely to remember that there was ever a problem. This is an area for fruitful brainstorming and cross-training involving the whole office. You will want to develop some policies by yourself, but every person connected with the office can get involved. Start with a brainstorming free-for-all in which any suggestion, no matter how crazy, is accepted for consideration. Set a few brainstorming rules, such as the following:

- No one is allowed to criticize, laugh at or disagree with any suggestion for at least the first 30 minutes of brainstorming.
- Record all ideas on paper for use in later discussions.
- Allow any suggestion to be made, whether it is a statement of a problem or a statement of a solution.

309. *Play the anticipation game.*   This is where you enlist the support of the staff and customers to look for potential problems and ask "What can go wrong here?" over and over until you find five or six things that need to be corrected before they become problems. It is easy to wait for customers to identify problems, but what if you can find a few yourself? Why wait for customers to tell you? Correct the problems now and ensure the happiness of your customers.

310. *Solicit first impressions.*   Ask someone who has never been to your office to come in posing as a customer. You'll want this "mystery shopper" to tell you his or her first impressions of your office. You'll find that you will get more useful information from the mystery shopper if you ask him or her to focus on specific aspects of your office, such as cleanliness, atmosphere, comfort, and staff attitudes and responsiveness. I strongly suggest that the mystery shopper go through the whole purchase experience. Later, invite this person to a staff meeting to present his or her findings. This will make for interesting discussions and successful problem-solving efforts.

311. *Discover common customer frustrations.*   This is another brainstorming session in which all employees are given a chance to mention the times they have observed frustrated customers. It may help to give an assignment ahead of time to get employees looking for signs of frustration in customers. During the discussion, ask the employees to describe specific customer behaviors they have observed.

This is a valuable training tool in itself. This awareness-building session can turn into a problem-solving session. Remember that feelings are the flags of happy and unhappy customers. Find out what causes their frustrations, make necessary corrections and you will have happy customers. Find out what makes them happy and satisfied and you will improve your reputation.

312. *Review existing policies and procedures.*   It may be difficult to see how policies and procedures create unhappy customers, but they are the single largest hidden cause of customer dissatisfaction. Without addressing these areas, you may be treating the symptoms of dissatisfaction without getting to the root of the problem. Whatever you do, don't skip this review process. The reviews should be done at least twice a year during a formal staff meeting. As an alternative, you may want to review at least one policy page and one procedure page from your manual during every staff meeting. Ask the following questions:

- What is working?
- What are we doing that differs from what we were doing last year?
- Where are the red flags that show things are not working as we wish?
- What needs to be improved so that customers are served better and our reputation is enhanced?

313. *Sharpen conflict resolution skills.*   Here is another practical training program in which everyone can get involved and practice actual skills, such as how to handle an angry customer or an angry coworker. You may want to get some outside help on this one. Call a local university or psychologists' group and ask for someone to come at no charge for this training.

314. *Review word-of-mouth marketing tactics.*   You cannot repeat this one too often. Staff members need to be reminded of the specific and important reasons your office is involved with word-of-mouth marketing. The follow-up training can focus on stopping negative word of mouth or promoting positive word of mouth. Remind staff members of the specific action steps you use. Get their feedback on how well they think word-of-mouth marketing is working.

Profiles Of Success

Bubbling Bath Spa & Tub
Rockville, Maryland

Business Profile: Bubbling Bath Spa & Tub sells a variety of tubs and spas and related accessories. The company also provides complete repair services.

Word-of-Mouth Tactics: Barry Fribush, owner of the company, has a few unchanging rules for building his business. His company is quickly available to service any spa located in his trading area, whether he sold the spa or not. When his company is called to service a spa sold by a competitor, he makes sure that the service personnel challenge themselves to give a higher level of service than the competitor gives. Fribush further ensures customer satisfaction by selling only the two or three spas that have proven track records for fewest breakdowns and service problems.

Customers participate in a scripted sales process that helps them compare the quality of Bubbling Bath Spa's products and services with competing alternatives. When a new spa is installed, the quality-assurance manager provides the customer with a thorough demonstration of the product. During the installation, the manager makes note of any items that need to be changed to make the system work perfectly. Once the system is working to perfection and the customer has been oriented, the quality-assurance manager asks the customer for the names of friends or relatives who might be interested in installing a spa. For every referral his company receives that results in a spa sale, the referring customer receives a finder's fee.

When a spa is installed, the installation crew distributes fliers in the neighborhood telling other homeowners about the event. The fliers bear the name of the installation supervisor, who receives a bonus for every spa sold as a result of the flier distribution.

One day Fribush went to a few auto dealers located near his spa showroom. He made arrangements to have Bubbling Bath Spa's discount coupons given to all customers of the dealer's service department. The coupon stated that it was provided courtesy of the auto dealer. Customers were encouraged to visit the spa showroom while they waited for their car to be repaired. Fribush has sold scores of spas to these auto service customers. The service managers like the program because it keeps customers pleasantly occupied while their cars are being serviced.

***Results*:** Word of mouth accounts for 72 percent of all new business coming into Bubbling Bath Spa & Tub. Owners of other businesses visit Fribush's business to analyze why the company continues to be so successful. *(Used by permission from Bubbling Bath Spa & Tub)*

Chapter 16

53 Places Where Word of Mouth Pays Immediate Dividends

"The product that will not sell without advertising will not sell profitably with advertising."

— *Albert Lasker*

*O*pportunities for launching word-of-mouth marketing campaigns abound. Whether you are trying word of mouth for the first time or have had success in this arena before, you should consider beefing up your word-of-mouth tactics when one of these opportunities comes your way. If you find that you have let word-of-mouth marketing opportunities slip by in the past, just look around and you will find another opportunity staring you in the face.

The pace of change in most industries leaves marketers breathless from just trying to keep up. Industry volatility is itself an opportunity for word-of-mouth promotion (see item 52 below). What other times are good? The following list will help you identify these opportunities so they don't pass you by.

Times To Implement a Word-of-Mouth Advertising Campaign

1. ***When the cost of paid advertising is very high for the market you are trying to reach.*** I never recommend that a company completely rule out paid advertising. However, when the cost of advertising for your product or service is excessively high, you should consider implementing a word-of-mouth ad-

vertising campaign. Launching such a program will encourage you to focus on the elements of the market (usually the opinion leaders and market mavens) that will return the most for what you spend. Word-of-mouth advertising will tap into the natural flow of communications.

2. ***When your product or service is difficult to describe to the consumer.*** If you have never been to the new restaurant in town, you are probably curious about how others rate it. You need help in understanding many other products and services with which you have no experience. It's human nature to turn to someone else for advice. There comes a point in the decision process that you don't want to read the advertising and the self-promoting information of the new restaurant. You want to know what someone else in your position has to say. What was it like? How was the service? How was the food? How were the prices?

3. ***When you need face-to-face communication with prospective customers.*** Many businesses require face-to-face communication with customers in order to complete the transaction. If you manage one of these businesses, word of mouth is the type of promotion best suited to your company. Your clients need to know something about you before they decide. They need to develop trust in you and your reliability. One way this can be accomplished is through personal communication with those who have firsthand knowledge of your product or service.

4. ***When new business depends upon professional referrals.*** Professional referral business is a natural fit with your word-of-mouth advertising. If you can name at least one other professional who shares your clients, you need to have a word-of-mouth marketing program in place.

5. ***When your product or service is highly intangible.*** The more intangible a product or service, the more prospective customers will need to hear about it from someone they know. You use tangible evidence in your other promotional methods, but consumers will likely depend upon the word of someone else before they buy.

6. ***When the degree of consumer involvement in the purchase decision is high.***   High consumer involvement means that the consumer commits significant personal or company resources to gather information about products, process that information and make the decision about the product. As the importance of the product increases, so does the degree of consumer involvement. As the expense of the product increases, so does the degree of consumer involvement. And as the complexity of the product increases, so does consumer involvement.

7. ***When there is a high perceived risk in using or buying your product or service.***   A maxim of marketing is that consumers want to get value equal or greater than their money and they want to avoid loss through a dissatisfying purchase experience. Some products and services are perceived by consumers to be high-risk. Maybe the product is new. Maybe the consumer has heard disparaging comments about the product from others. Or maybe the financial investment is significant. To manage their risks, consumers depend on the word of someone else before making this type of purchase decision.

8. ***When you desire slow, steady growth.***   Word of mouth usually works in a steady, methodical way, except for highly unusual (fad) products or unusual situations (the appearance of a celebrity at your place of business). But if you are operating the right program, you will always have a steady stream of business from word of mouth.

9. ***When your company or your personal reputation is very important to the consumer.***   Many business owners have an intuitive sense when their reputation is the most important issue to consumers. If you are in a purchase situation or in a company where this is true for you, word of mouth is the key element that will help the customer succeed through the purchase process.

10. ***When you take a low-price leadership position in the market.***   Low price is one of the most important dynamics in word of mouth. Because price is central to what the product means,

information about a low price is likely to be transferred to prospective customers. You can be guaranteed that in this type of situation, word of mouth is occurring.

11. ***When you take the quality leadership position in the market.*** Just as low price sparks movement through the grapevine, so does high quality. This is the other side of the price = quality equation, and is at the core of what the product means for the consumer. If you have the highest quality product in your industry or territory, exploit this by promoting through word of mouth.

12. ***When you are targeting a narrow-market niche.*** When you are attempting to reach a narrow niche, mass communication is overkill. Word of mouth will target your desired customers effectively. Used in conjunction with direct marketing, word of mouth is the most powerful promotion method.

13. ***When you need endorsements for your product or service.*** Endorsements from a celebrity (local, regional or national) add energy to word of mouth. However, don't stop at hiring a celebrity. Your word-of-mouth marketing program needs to be integrated with all your promotion tactics. Above all, avoid the error of thinking that a celebrity endorsement will make up for what your champion customers can do for you. As powerful as they are, celebrity endorsements are impersonal forms of communication when used in mass advertising. The word of a satisfied champion customer, however, is a powerful form of personal communication.

14. ***When the consumer has a difficult time differentiating between your company or product and competitors.*** Your first task is to find or create a unique advantage that sets you apart from competitors. If you are not sure what that is, ask your champion clients for their opinion. Your next task is to develop a strong word-of-mouth marketing program that capitalizes on the ability of champion clients to describe your best qualities to others. When differentiation is difficult to achieve in an advertisement, your champion clients can explain it in their own words.

15. ***When you have a known negative image among target consumers or in any group.*** The first hint of negative image should spur you to action. The longer you wait, the more damaging negative talk will be. Recognize that, as a business owner, you may be the *last* to find out about your negative image. If you brush off reports of negative word of mouth and don't take immediate corrective action, your business will continue to suffer.

16. ***When you operate within a stagnant industry with ho-hum attitudes of both consumers and producers.*** Word of mouth can be one of the most dynamic competitive strategies in this situation. Promotions have the power to create competitive advantage and position in the mind of the customer. While mass, impersonal advertising can accomplish this, it is risky. Word-of-mouth promotion, on the other hand, is much less risky. Why? Because word of mouth is inseparable from product, pricing and distribution issues.

17. ***When you want to leverage your distribution channel relationships.*** Distribution channels foster word-of-mouth advertising. Most industries are so closely woven that something happening at one corner will immediately be known at the other corners. We know word of mouth happens in distribution channels. The task is to manage the process carefully to get positive results.

18. ***When you are introducing a new product into the market.*** New products and services are ideally suited for word of mouth. Consumers are on the lookout for new products, and opinion leaders are the people they look to for advice on new products. If you launch a new product without them, you are missing half the power of your promotion.

19. ***When you are attempting to revive a mature product.*** Products go through life cycles, just like people. As a product matures and declines, you can pull back on expensive paid advertising (an action that will improve your profitability) while emphasizing word of mouth. At this stage of the product's

life, repeat purchases are as important as the actions of first-time buyers.

20. ***When you need (for any reason) to use limited distribution of your product or service.***   There are many reasons for limited distribution, but usually it is because you don't have the money to establish wide distribution relationships. When this is the case, use word of mouth to get the product firmly established in one market. This will generate sales and the cash you'll need to widen your distribution efforts.

21. ***When you achieve a significant product innovation.***   True innovations are rare these days, but when you do have one, your word-of-mouth networks should be fired up to spread the news as quickly as possible. Diffusion of these types of innovations can achieve results as dramatic as for a brand new product.

22. ***When you have cut your advertising expenses during a recession.***   Some advertising agencies will counsel you *not* to cut your advertising expenses during a recession ("This is just the time to get ahead of your competitors..."). The reality is that most companies cut expenses during a recession. If you have to cut down to the bone, don't cut out word of mouth. Instead, rebuild your entire promotion budget around word of mouth and focus paid advertising on opinion leaders and marketing mavens.

23. ***When your advertising is shown to be ineffective in attracting new business.***   If you are experimenting with advertising tactics, start with your opinion leaders, then build an advertising program to complement the word of mouth.

24. ***When there is a strong human element in the product or service.***   People talk about people, things that happen to people, what people say, what people do, and how people react to situations and to others. This is the fodder for your word-of-mouth arsenal. If your business involves people to a great degree, word of mouth is very significant, and you should be managing the process carefully.

25. ***When there is a high degree of contact between your company personnel and consumers.*** Word of mouth thrives on people issues. Whenever you have an opportunity to wield personal influence with an opinion leader, you are setting the word-of-mouth wheels in motion. Look at the structure of your company and tally the situations in which personal contact is integral to doing business. These are the opportunities to influence positive word of mouth.

26. ***When you start within a defined geographic area and build from there.*** Many start-up companies are forced, due to lack of resources, to gain a foothold in just one location. Success in one market opens up opportunities to expand to other markets, and word of mouth can play an important role in this success. If you start small, incorporate word-of-mouth principles with your promotion mix.

27. ***When your product or service touches any of the core elements of cultural expression (fashion, food, entertainment, etc.).*** Word of mouth is essentially the transfer of the meaning of a product from one satisfied user to another person. When the product involves a highly valued expression of culture, word-of-mouth dynamics are guaranteed to be a part of the experience. If your product is related to any cultural trait (food, language, clothing, implements, art forms), you are missing the most powerful form of signaling by not managing word of mouth.

28. ***When you are attempting to reach a strong, cohesive social group.*** Talk is what binds social groups together. It fuels expansion and group success. If you are targeting a clearly defined social group, like it or not, word of mouth will happen. Your task is to manage the process to achieve the most desired effects.

29. ***When your product or company has a clearly defined position in the mind of the consumer.*** Position is what consumers collectively give you and your company in relation to competi-

tors. They do this by talking or writing about you to one another. If you have a clearly defined position in the market, this means that word-of-mouth dynamics are already at work. It also means that with a little management, you can positively influence that word of mouth to bring in more business.

30. ***When you want to boast that your business comes primarily from referrals of satisfied customers.*** Entrepreneurial ego is no laughing matter in business. It is the power behind the dream of success. Face your ego drive and use it to your advantage. If you really want a referral-based business, grapevine marketing is your only promotion method.

31. ***When you know your consumers have strong emotions regarding your product or service before, during or after purchase.*** Emotions are the rocket engines of word of mouth. If your employees tell you that consumers are showing their feelings (whether positive or negative), it should be a flag to you that word of mouth is happening. Jump-start a word-of-mouth campaign and see the results unfold before your eyes.

32. ***When your competitors use unethical practices.*** In some industries, ethical behavior is a differentiational strategy. Unethical activities are so rampant in some sections of the economy that you can set yourself apart from your competitors with consistent attention to ethical behavior. Others in the industry infrastructure will notice and will talk about it.

33. ***When you are attempting to reach an ethnic subgroup in the community.*** Word of mouth is at the core of ethnic communication patterns. If you ignore this vital avenue of influence, you will fight an uphill battle to overcome cultural barriers.

34. ***When you want the distribution channel intermediaries to talk about your product or service.*** One of the most important "push" strategies is to have a well-managed word-of-mouth marketing program. Add word-of-mouth tactics to your rebates,

discounts, retailer support and return guarantees, and you will enjoy channel relationships that are productive.

35. *When you consider using word of mouth for the first time.* Now is the time to act on your intuition. If you delay, you will miss an opportunity.

36. *When you want to coordinate your internal promotion with your external promotion.* Make word of mouth the basis from which to build this coordinated management effort. The more visible, glamorous promotion methods will get their share of your budget. What you need is a thorough word-of-mouth effort focused on opinion leaders, marketing mavens and influentials. Put it in your budget. Assign it to someone to manage, and watch the synergism happen.

37. *When you have difficulty dividing your market into the traditional market segments.* For some businesses, market segmentation is difficult. If you are in this situation, start with the word-of-mouth segments. Start with opinion leaders, market mavens and influentials, and note the clients they refer to you. In other words, let the word-of-mouth segments inform you regarding the other segments based on demographics, benefits, user characteristics, etc.

38. *When you want prospective consumers to know who your valued customers are.* I've heard many business owners say, "If the public only knew who we served, they would be surprised." If you have said this (at least to yourself), act on it with a consistent word-of-mouth marketing program. The public will not only be surprised at your clientele, they also will be impressed. They will want your products, too.

39. *When you think word of mouth may be happening in your business but aren't sure where or when it is happening.* I know many businesses in this situation. If you think it is true for your situation, it is time to set up a word-of-mouth marketing program so you can determine when it happens and track the

impact. This should be one of the strongest encouragements to you that you can make it work more if you pay a little attention to it.

40. ***When you can't think of the names of more than one or two loyal customers who tell others about your company.*** This is an indicator that, as a business manager, you are not aware of the word-of-mouth dynamics already at work. You should study the referral patterns by asking consumers who told them about your business and chart these patterns.

41. ***When you have high employee turnover.*** High employee turnover may indicate high customer turnover. If this is true, be warned that word of mouth is the knot at the end of your rope. Not only will positive word of mouth help you recruit employees, it will also help you decrease turnover rates and build loyal consumers.

42. ***When you are ready to hire a new employee.*** There is much to think about when recruiting a new employee, but a major consideration should be the candidate's word-of-mouth marketing capabilities. Here is the simple question: Do you want employees who support word of mouth or who undermine it? Recruit, select and hire with this in mind.

43. ***When you refer a customer to another company.*** Sending a customer away is not always the most pleasant experience. However, it is an opportunity to enhance word of mouth. By your words and tone of voice, you can build confidence in the company to which you refer your customer. You can also follow up with that company to confirm that your customer achieved his or her goals. Making a smooth transition for your client says a lot about your professionalism. It will spark a conversation between your client and others.

44. ***When you are not sure how your new customers heard about your business.*** When this is the case, simply ask who told them about you. Although it is not the whole program, this will

get your word-of-mouth efforts going in the right direction. You can then continue the program by encouraging your champion customers to make referrals. Give them more information about your company. See that their personal experiences with your company are positive, and thank them when they refer others to you.

45. ***When a new competitor enters your territory.***   In response to competition, you can slash your prices, come out with innovations, pump up paid advertising—all of which may make it more difficult for a new competitor to succeed. Positive word of mouth, however, is your best defense. Goodwill and reputation are the only things competitors cannot steal from you.

46. ***When you are the biggest company in your industry or in your territory.***   Size is often correlated with sluggishness and unresponsiveness in American business. You can overcome these liabilities by developing a word-of-mouth program that keeps you in touch with consumers. If you are the big company in your area, use this leverage to get people talking positively about you. Make sure you have something of substance behind the word of mouth. Nothing can kill a word-of-mouth program like shallowness.

47. ***When you are the smallest company in your industry or in your territory.***   Being small has its liabilities, too. You don't have the cash to put into paid advertising like the big companies do. You don't have the people (and the corresponding overhead) to represent your interests. Word of mouth is one of your best allies in this situation. Because you cannot afford to waste your promotion dollars, you will see every champion customer as your lifeline to success. Organize a word-of-mouth marketing program and leverage every opinion leader you can reach.

48. ***When you want to change the rules of competition in your industry or in your territory.***   Competitive strategy often calls

for changing the rules of competition. As risky as this is, sometimes you have to do it. At times these changes are accomplished without fanfare, but often promotion is needed to help signal the change when it is important to consumers. If this is the case, use word of mouth to reach the public.

49. ***When you are attempting to reach a very small market.*** Just like reaching a narrow market calls for word of mouth, so does reaching a small market. Why would you want to spend a fortune on mass-media advertising to reach less than 1 percent of the market? It makes more sense to carefully select the opinion leaders who are connected to this small market and promote your product through them.

50. ***When you are attempting to reach the affluent.*** Here is another example of why word of mouth is so powerful. You can reach influentials through their opinion leaders—other influentials. Placing paid advertisements in selected media can help, but remember that talk among these people is what makes the difference.

51. ***When you want to increase your profits.*** Profitability is directly correlated with positive word of mouth. As you add value to your products and services by fostering word of mouth, you will have consumers willing to pay more. You will spend less on paid advertising (which translates into higher profits), and you will build a long-term advantage over competitors. Brand loyalty will be created, which, again, translates into higher profits for you.

52. ***When your competitor's product or service does not have a clearly defined brand image.*** Brand image is the source of one of the most subtle differences between products. Using intuition, customers can tell the difference. The opportunity to build word of mouth exists when the competitor's product has a blurred image or is inconsistent with its promotional messages. In these circumstances, jump on the opportunity by first making

sure that you have a strong position and a clearly defined image. Then exploit this opportunity by implementing some of the word-of-mouth tactics outlined in this book.

53. ***When your product must be accepted by each new generation.*** Parents and authority figures talk to children about what products are desirable. Schoolteachers, work supervisors and other role models are examples of individuals who influence younger generations. That primary influence is through word of mouth. Give these individuals plenty to talk about.

For your business, the best time to develop and implement a word-of-mouth marketing program is now. Now you can use the secrets of the best companies in the world. Now you can use the most natural form of promotion by tapping into the power of the grapevine. Now you can save money and get results. Now you can let your customers do the talking!

*B*ibliography

Books

Allport, G.W., and Postman, L. *The Psychology of Rumor.* New York: Holt Publishing, 1947.

Arndt, J. *Word-of-Mouth Advertising.* New York: Advertising Research Foundation, 1967.

Cafferky, M.E. *Patients Build Your Practice: Word-of-Mouth Marketing for Healthcare Practitioners.* New York: McGraw-Hill, 1994.

Davidson, J.P. *Marketing on a Shoestring.* New York: John Wiley & Sons, 1988, 27-39.

Fagen, R.R. "The Components of Communication Networks," in *Creating Social Change.* Zaltman, G., Kotler, P. and Kaufman, R., editors. New York: Holt, Rinehart & Winston, 1972, 223-33.

Harris, G. and Harris, G.J. *Talk Is Cheap.* Los Angeles: The Americas Group, 1991.

Kotler, P. *Marketing Management,* 8th ed. Englewood Cliffs, N.J.: Prentice-Hall, 1994.

Lauer, R.H. *Perspectives on Social Change,* 4th ed. Boston: Allyn & Bacon, 1991.

Lowery, S. and DeFleur, M.L. *Milestones in Mass Communications Research.* New York: Longman, 1983, 176-203.

McKenna, R. *Relationship Marketing.* Reading, Mass.: Addison-Wesley Publishing Co., 1991.

217

O'Shaughnessy, J. *Explaining Buyer Behavior*. New York: Oxford University Press, 1992.

Ostrow, R. and Smith, S.R. *The Dictionary of Marketing*. New York: Fairchild Publications, 1988, 171, 257.

Phillips, M. and Rasberry, S. *Marketing Without Advertising*. Berkeley, Calif.: Nolo Press, 1990.

Porter, M. *Competitive Advantage*. New York: The Free Press, 1985.

Roane, S. *The Secrets of Savvy Networking*. New York: Warner Books, 1993.

Robertson, T.S. and Kassarjian, H. *Handbook of Consumer Behavior*. New York: Prentice-Hall, 1991.

Rogers, E.M. *Communication of Innovations*, 2d ed. New York: The Free Press, 1971.

Schnaars, S.P. *Marketing Strategy: A Customer-Driven Approach*. New York: The Free Press, 1991.

Schiffman, L.G. and Kanuk, L.L. *Consumer Behavior*, 3d ed. New York: Prentice-Hall, 1987.

Sewell, C. *Customers for Life*. New York: Simon & Schuster, 1991.

Wilson, J. *Word of Mouth Marketing*. New York: John Wiley & Sons, 1991.

Magazine Articles

Arndt, J. "Role of Product-Related Conversations in the Diffusion of a New Product." *Journal of Marketing Research*, vol. 4, no. 3, Aug. 1967, 291-95.

Atkin, C. and Block, M. "Effectiveness of Celebrity Endorsers." *Journal of Advertising Research*, vol. 23, no. 1, Feb./March 1983, 57-61.

Baumgarten, S.A. "The innovative communicator in the diffusion process." *Journal of Marketing Research*, vol. 12, no. 1, Feb. 1975, 12-18.

Bloch, P.H. "The product enthusiast: implications for marketing strategy." *Journal of Consumer Marketing*, vol. 3, no. 3, Summer 1986, 51-62.

Brooks Jr., R.C. "Word-of-mouth advertising in selling new products." *Journal of Marketing*, vol. 22, no. 2, Oct. 1957, 154-61.

Brown, J.J. and Reingen, P.H. "Social Ties and Word-of-Mouth Referral Behavior." *Journal of Consumer Research*, vol. 14, no. 3, Dec. 1987, 350-62.

Buckner, H.T. "A theory of rumor transmission." *Public Opinion Quarterly*, vol. 29, no. 1, 1965, 54-70.

Cafferky, M.E. "Market Your Center Without Spending a Cent." *Early Childhood News,* March/April 1993, 26-27.

Cafferky, M.E. "Build Enrollment by Word of Mouth." *Dance Teacher Now,* vol. 15, no. 7, Sept. 1993, 29-32.

Chan, K.K. and Misra, S. "Characteristics of the opinion leader: a new dimension." *Journal of Advertising,* vol. 19, no. 3, 1990, 53-60.

Davidow, W.H. and Uttal, B. "Coming: the customer service decade." *Across the Board,* vol. 26, no. 11, Nov. 1989, 33-37.

Dichter, E. "How Word-of-Mouth Advertising Works." *Harvard Business Review,* vol. 44, no. 6, Nov./Dec. 1966, 147-66.

Engel, J.F., Kegerreis, R.J. and Blackwell, R.D. "Word-of-Mouth Communication by the Innovator." *Journal of Marketing,* vol. 33, no. 3, July 1969, 15-19.

Feick, L.F. and Price, L.L. "The Market Maven: A diffuser of marketplace information." *Journal of Marketing,* vol. 51, no. 1, Jan. 1987, 83-87.

Friedman, H.H. and Friedman, L. "Endorser Effectiveness by Product Type." *Journal of Advertising Research,* vol. 19, no. 5, Oct. 1979, 63-71.

Hastings, H. "Introducing New Products Without Advertising." *Journal of Consumer Behavior,* vol. 7, no. 3, Summer 1990, 19-25.

Haywood, K.M. "Managing Word-of-Mouth Communications." *Journal of Services Marketing,* vol. 3, no. 2, Spring 1989, 55-67.

Herr, P.M., Kardes, F.R. and Kim, J. "Effects of Word-of-Mouth and Product-Attribute Information on Persuasion: An Accessibility-Diagnosticity Perspective." *Journal of Consumer Research,* vol. 17, no. 4, March 1991, 454-62.

Iacobucci, D. and Hopkins, N. "Modeling Dyadic Interactions and Networks in Marketing." *Journal of Marketing Research,* vol. 29, no. 1, Feb. 1992, 5-17.

Kamen, J.M., Azhari, A.C. and Kragh, J.R. "What a spokesman does for a sponsor." *Journal of Advertising Research,* vol. 15, no. 2, April 1975, 17-24.

Katz, E. "The two-step flow of communication: an up-to-date report on an hypothesis." *Public Opinion Quarterly,* vol. 21, no. 1, Spring 1957, 61-78.

King, C.W. and Summers. J.O. "Overlap of opinion leadership across consumer product categories." *Journal of Marketing Research,* vol. 7, no. 1, Feb. 1970, 43-50.

Kotler, P. and Zaltman, G. "Targeting prospects for a new product." *Journal of Advertising Research,* vol. 16, no. 1, Feb. 1976, 7-18.

Landler, M., Konrad, W., Schiller, Z. and Therrien, L. "What Happened to Advertising?" *Business Week,* Sept. 23, 1991.

Leonard-Barton, D. "Experts as Negative Opinion Leaders in the Diffusion of a Technological Innovation." *Journal of Consumer Research,* vol. 11, no. 4, March 1985, 914-26.

Mancuso, J.R. "Why not create opinion leaders for new product introductions?" *Journal of Marketing,* vol. 33, no. 3, July 1969, 20-25.

McCracken, G. "Who Is the Celebrity Endorser? Cultural Foundations of the Endorsement Process." *Journal of Consumer Research,* vol. 16, no. 3, Dec. 1989, 310-21.

Montgomery, D.B. and Silk, A.J. "Clusters of consumer interests and opinion leaders' spheres of influence." *Journal of Marketing Research,* vol. 8, no. 3, Aug. 1971, 317-21.

Myers, J.H. and Robertson, T.S. "Dimensions of opinion leadership." *Journal of Marketing Research,* vol. 9, no. 1, Feb. 1972, 41-46.

Piirto, R. "The Influentials." *American Demographics,* vol. 14, no. 10, Oct. 1992, 30-38.

Plymire, J. "Complaints as Opportunities." *Journal of Services Marketing,* vol. 8, no. 2, Spring 1991, 39-43.

Reichheld, F.F. and Sasser, W.E. "Zero defections: Quality comes to services." *Harvard Business Review,* Sept./Oct. 1990, 301-07.

Richins, M.L. "Negative word-of-mouth by dissatisfied consumers: A pilot study." *Journal of Marketing,* vol. 47, no. 1, Winter 1983, 68-78.

Robertson, T.S. "The process of innovation and the diffusion of innovations." *Journal of Marketing,* vol. 31, no. 1, Jan. 1967, 14-19.

Schachter, S. and Burdick, H. "A field experiment on rumor transmission and distortion." *Journal of Abnormal and Social Psychology,* vol. 50, no. 3, May 1955, 363-71.

Sheth, J.N. "Word-of-mouth in low-risk innovations." *Journal of Advertising Research,* vol. 11, no. 3, June 1971, 15-18.

Waldrop, J. "Educating the customer." *American Demographics,* vol. 13, no. 9, Sept. 1991, 44-47.

Weimann, G. "The influentials: back to the concept of opinion leaders?" *Public Opinion Quarterly,* vol. 55, no. 2, Summer 1991, 267-79.

Whyte, W.H. "The Web of Word of Mouth." *Fortune,* vol. 50, no. 5, Nov. 1954, 140-43, 204-12.

Yavas, U., Luqmani, M. and Quraeshi, A.Z. "Facilitating the adoption of information technology in a developing country." *Information and Management,* vol. 23, no. 2, Aug. 1992, 75-82.

$\mathcal{I}$ndex

221